Things that matter

By the same author

What's your opinion?
Link up

Things that matter

Philip Grosset

Evans Brothers Limited, London

Published by Evans Brothers Limited
Montague House, Russell Square, London, WC1

First published 1966
Reprinted 1969
Reprinted 1970
Reprinted 1971

Printed in Great Britain by
Lewis Reprints Limited, London and Tonbridge
Limp 237 28327 1
Cased 237 28891 5   PRA 2609

Contents

Contents

Acknowledgments

For permission to quote from copyright material in this book, the author and publishers are indebted to: George Allen & Unwin Limited for an extract from *My Life and Thought* by Albert Schweitzer; W. H. Allen & Company for 'On Saturday Afternoon' published with *The Loneliness of the Long Distance Runner* by Alan Sillitoe; *Amateur Cine World* and Mr Tony Rose for an extract from his article on film censorship of 20 May 1965; *Bath Evening Chronicle* for the article 'Planned fire to repay teacher'; BBC for an extract from a condensed version from *The Listener* of 'The Conscience of the Programme Director', an address given by Sir Hugh Greene; Beat Publications Limited for extracts from *The Beatles Book*; Geoffrey Bles Limited for extracts from J. B. Phillips' translation of the *New Testament*; The Bodley Head Limited for an extract from *The Story of Insulin* by Professor G. A. Wrenshall, Dr G. Hetenyi and Dr W. R. Feasby; Jonathan Cape Limited for an extract from *Catch 22* by Joseph Heller; Central Board of Finance of the Church of England for extracts from the *Prayer Book, 1928*; Chatto & Windus Limited for an extract from *The Insecure Offenders* by T. R. Fyvel; Jonathan Clowes Limited for extracts from *Love Me Do* by Michael Braun; *The Daily Mirror* for the Andy Capp cartoons; *The Daily Telegraph* and Mr Edward Jeffrey for his article 'Face to Face with a Titan Missile'; Gerald Duckworth & Company Limited for an extract from *Teenage Tyranny* by Grace and Fred M. Hechtinger; Encyclopaedia Britannica Limited for two extracts (see 'Censorship' and 'Woman's Place'); Eyre & Spottiswoode (Publishers) Limited for an extract from its *Book of Common Prayer, 1662*; Frederic Fell, USA for extract from *Auschwitz* by Dr Miklos Nyiszli; Fleetway Publications Limited for *Treasure Convoy*; Victor Gollancz Limited for an extract from *Profiles of the Future* by Arthur C. Clarke, and an extract from *The Man Who Won the Pools* by J. I. M. Stewart; Heinemann Educational Books Limited for an extract from *The Living Theatre* by Elmer Rice; Hodder & Stoughton Limited for an extract from *The Right to Life* by Norman St. John-Stevas; HMSO for an extract from *Britain: An Official Handbook,* and for an extract from *Command Paper 2641*, Report of the Departmental Committee on experiments on animals, April, 1965; Hutchinson & Company (Publishers) Limited for an extract from *The Courage of his Convictions* by Tony Parker; Michael Joseph Limited for 'Compassion Circuit' from *The Seeds of Time* by John Wyndham; William Kimber & Company Limited for an extract from the foreword to *The Destruction of Dresden* by David Irving; *The Lancet* for the article on 'Acute phosgene poisoning'; *The Listener* and Mr Wilfred

De'Ath for extracts from his article 'Just Me and Nobody Else'; Longmans Green & Company Limited for an extract from *In Flanders Fields* by Leon Wolff; Macdonald & Company (Publishers) Limited for an extract from *The Big Switch* by Muriel Box; Macmillan Company for extracts from *The Psychology of Adolescence* by Dr Arthur T. Jersild; Bryan McAllister for the two cartoons drawn specially for this book; Methuen & Company Limited for an extract from *The Child Who Never Grew* by Pearl S. Buck; Ministry of Defence for the RAF Advertisement; Brian Morris for *Genesis*; George Newnes Limited for an extract from *Pop Pics Super*; *New Statesman* for 'Incendiary' by Vernon Scannell; *Observer Foreign News Service* for an extract from a report by Stanley Karnow, issued on 30 April, 1965; Penguin Books Limited for the extracts from *The Film and the Public* by Roger Manvell, from *Discrimination and Popular Culture* edited by Denys Thompson, from *Suicide and Attempted Suicide* by Erwin Stengel, and from *Crime in a Changing Society* by Howard Jones; Laurence Pollinger Limited and the Estate of the late Mrs Frieda Lawrence for *Censors* and *Conundrum* by D. H. Lawrence; *Punch* for 'Once I built a Pop Group' by Alan Coren, and for the Sprod cartoon; Routledge & Kegan Paul Limited for an extract from *This is Your Child* by A. Allen and A. Morton, and an extract from *Handbook of Social Psychology* by Kimball Young; Michael Schofield for an extract from the article in *The Sunday Times*, taken from his book *The Sexual Behaviour of Young People* published by Longmans Green & Company Limited; Scorpion Press for the poem *Your Attention Please* by Peter Porter; Scottish Society for the Prevention of Vivisection for the pamphlet on *Vivisection*; *She* for the article 'One Doctor's Opinion'; *Sunday Express* for Giles cartoons; *The Sunday Times* for an extract from an 'Insight' feature; Tandem Books Limited for extracts from *Generation X* by Charles Hamblett and Jane Deverson; *The Times Educational Supplement* for the Robot cartoon; Weidenfeld & Nicolson Limited for an extract from *At Your Peril* by Hugh Cudlipp; The World's Work Limited for an extract from *Good Manners in a Nutshell* by Sally Hines.

Introduction

The main aim of this anthology is to provide material for discussion. However, it is hoped that it may also prove of interest to the general reader.

Suggestions for discussion leaders and a list of recommended films will be found at the end of the book.

PHILIP GROSSET

1 The war game

Flanders 1917

This is a description of trench warfare in the
First World War (1914–1918):

The stretcher-bearers first retrieved the seriously wounded
British; then the moderately wounded British; then the
British dead; then the German lightly wounded. The German seriously wounded mostly had to be ignored, and enemy
dead in No-Man's-Land were never touched by British
bearers except for souvenirs. While on an individual basis the
campaign was fought by both armies with reasonable
decency, sometimes hideously wounded men found lying on
the battlefield were mercifully shot by their opponents.
In one reported instance a British officer scouting the area
came across an enemy soldier mangled but still alive. 'Shoot
him,' he said unhappily to his runner, as the German lay
watching them in a stupor of agony. The runner unslung
his rifle but could not fire, nor could another soldier in the
little patrol. The officer drew his own pistol, stared in gloom
at the German writhing on the ground below; and could do
no more. Later he said savagely; 'Damn funny, wasn't it?
And we just left him there, so I suppose he'll die in the mud
tonight.'

One photograph shows six stretcher-bearers carrying one
wounded soldier back from the front. The bearers, up to
mud from one's ankles to another's hips, seem to be smiling
almost apologetically. All day the walking wounded in their
bandages drifted back, punctured and lacerated in the usual
ways of war, trudging along the porridge-like roads in their
heavy boots which resembled nothing but blobs of mud.
(Some got lost at night and walked the wrong way—directly
back into the wire.) At regimental-aid posts, only a few
hundred feet rearward, doctors worked swiftly at routine
first-aid or serious amputations required on the spot. Then
the men were passed back to another dressing station, except
for those still needing surgery, who were moved to a Casualty

Clearing Station. At these collecting points the ambulances lined up by the hundreds like taxis at the Waldorf—waiting and loading and rattling through the area all day and night with their sodden cargoes. The men moaned or lay half stunned during the clattery ride back to hospital, where they would variously find peace or permanent disability, or an anti-climactic death after all.

But many of the lightly wounded were more cheerful, and joked about small injuries which meant a soft life for months, perhaps a permanent assignment in 'Blighty'. Unlike these gay chaps were the majority of silent, brooding ones who sat covered with whitish clay, staring at charcoal stoves and waiting for ambulances. In some the spirit of soldiery sometimes still flickered, and at least one remarked sullenly, 'Only the mud beat us. We should have gone much further except for the mud.'

At the roadside dressing stations danger was not yet past, for still the Germans probed the roads and intersections with their long-range guns. Doctors themselves were killed there, and the wounded were sometimes wounded again, or finally finished off for good. At these collecting points around Broodseinde, Poelcapelle, along the Menin Road and beside the Ypres-Staden railway, the wounded congregated crying and moaning so that the sound rang in everyone's ears all day and destroyed many an appetite. And later in the day and evening some of the dead began to be hauled back in mummy-like blankets ready for burial. Pitifully small they seemed, hardly half the size of the cursing, burly fellows (four per corpse) that slid and stumbled down the tracks with their tolerant burdens.

In No-Man's-Land the wounded still lay in the mud. Their shouting and sobbing kept everyone's nerves on edge. Those in shellholes generally drowned there. Slowly they slipped down the muddy banks into the water below, too weak to hold themselves up. Their feeble whispers often could not be heard by comrades passing by. As time went on No-Man's-Land thus became converted into a vast limbo of abandoned dead and dying. Each shellhole with blood on its water usually meant another corpse entombed below.

Unfortunately the harried stretcher-bearers had encouraged the wounded to try to make their own way back. Hundreds started off, but could not keep going. Exhausted and losing blood they crawled into shellholes, only to learn that this blunder would cost them their lives. Battlefield deaths of this kind are described by a survivor:

. . . a khaki-clad leg, three heads in a row, the rest of the bodies submerged, giving one the idea that they had used their last ounce of strength to keep their heads above the rising water. In another miniature pond, a hand still gripping a rifle is all that is visible, while its next-door neighbour is occupied by a steel helmet and half a head, the staring eyes glaring icily at the green slime which floats on the surface almost at their level.

The drier portions of the battlefield held more orthodox collections of dead: one German was pinned to the ground by a bayonet around which his hands had stiffened as he tried to withdraw it. A corporal's trousers had been blown off and his belly ripped open up to the chest. The top of a machine-gunner's head was missing, and his shoulders and gun coated with blood. One corpse was so strangely battered that nobody could understand what had happened. Many hundreds bore tiny perforations not visible beneath their uniforms. Machine-gunners lay scarcely relaxed beside their machines—hard, grim fighting men still facing the enemy British. A few were fearfully butchered by near hits of large shells. The faces of the dead everywhere were brown and aghast, their white teeth always showing.

. . . The war ended at the eleventh hour of the eleventh day of the eleventh month of 1918. It had meant nothing, solved nothing, and proved nothing; and in so doing had killed 8,538,315 men and variously wounded 21,219,452. Of 7,750,919 others taken prisoner or missing, well over a million were later presumed dead; thus the total deaths (not counting civilians) approach ten million. The moral and mental defects of the leaders of the human race had been demonstrated with some exactitude. One of them (Woodrow Wilson) later admitted that the war had been fought for business interests; another (David Lloyd George) had told a newspaperman: 'If people really knew, the war would be stopped tomorrow, but of course they don't—and can't know. The correspondents don't write and the censorship

3

wouldn't pass the truth. The thing is horrible, and beyond human nature to bear, and I feel I cannot go on any longer with the bloody business. . . .'

But now the thing was over. After a few final shells thrown into enemy lines at eleven o'clock by cannoneers who shall be for ever nameless, an uncanny silence enveloped the Western Front. Cautiously, unbelievingly, the men raised themselves above their trenches, shellholes, and dugouts, and stared at the opposing lines. Soon they became very excited, and often regrettably drunk; and, as the once-hostile armies merged, the men exchanged cigarettes, wine, embraces and souvenirs. Then came the stern, inevitable order forbidding fraternisation.

From *In Flanders Fields* by Leon Wolff

The First World War. After a gas attack.

Treasure Convoy

Here is an extract from a war comic read by older teenagers. The story is set in Yugoslavia which was invaded by
the Germans in 1941. The main characters are:

Wing Commander Rusty Braddon. England's 'ace of
aces'. He has landed his Spitfire in order to help Yugoslav
patriots recapture gold bars and Yugoslav hostages from
the Germans.

Rovnic and Salzan. Two of the Yugoslav patriots who
are being helped by Rusty Braddon.

Skalar. A Yugoslav traitor who has helped the Germans
but has also stolen two of the gold bars from them for
his own use. Together with a German officer, he has been
captured by Rusty Braddon and the Yugoslav patriots.

Now read down each row of pictures:

SALZAN SPUN THE WHEEL . . . AND THE LADEN VEHICLE SCREECHED AROUND THE TURNING ON TO THE HILL ROAD. THE SECOND CAPTURED LORRY FOLLOWED.

THANKS FOR THE LOAN — YOU CAN HAVE THIS BACK NOW.

BUT RUSTY BRADDON KNEW THAT THE GOLD LORRIES' SPEED WAS NOT ENOUGH. AND AS THEY THUNDERED AROUND THE BEND AND RACED TOWARDS THE ACE'S SPITFIRE . . .

I FEEL SAFER DRIVING MY OWN BUS ROVNIC — SEE YOU LATER!

THE DEADLY ACCURATE GRENADE ERUPTED WITH AN EAR-SHATTERING ROAR —

IN THREE EXPLOSIVE STRIDES, RUSTY WAS IN THE COCKPIT — THE GREAT ENGINE COUGHED, SPLUTTERED AND BROKE INTO EAR SPLITTING LIFE . . .

SHORTER THAN THE CARRIER'S FLIGHT DECK . . . SO IT'LL BE A RECORD OR BUST . . . UP YOU GROUND HUGGING BEAUTY, UP.

SLAM YOUR FOOT DOWN, ROVNIC — THE ARMOURED CARS ARE ON OUR TAIL AND HOPE YOUR OTHER LADS HAVE DONE THEIR STUFF.

WITH THE STICK IN THE PIT OF HIS STOMACH, RUSTY WATCHED THE BEND RUSH AT HIM. THEN, AT THE LAST MINUTE, THE PLANE LIFTED.

AS BRADDON SLID INTO THE CAB, THE TWO ESCAPING TRUCKS WERE FORCED TO SLOW DOWN. THEY HAD REACHED THE BOMB CRATER — ONLY THE HOLE HAD BEEN FILLED.

FIRST CLASS BIT OF ROAD MENDING. GET ABOARD CHAPS — AND FAST!

BUT IT ALSO HELPS THE GERMANS NOW WE DEPEND ON SPEED.

NOTHING COULD STOP THE SHATTERING COLLISION BETWEEN THE CARS AND THE AIRCRAFT — EXCEPT THE SUPERB SKILL OF RUSTY BRADDON! A FLICK OF THE CONTROLS — AND THE SPITFIRE SPUN OVER . . .

ROAD HOGS!

B

Face to face with a Titan Missile

Below is a factual account of a journalist's visit to a U.S. missile squadron:

We had driven over 50 miles southeast from Davis-Montham Air Force Base at Tucson across the Arizona desert to where, hidden below the desert floor, was poised a new weapon. Old stories of the Apache wars paled to fairy tale stuff at the thought of its power. We were going to see an operational intercontinental ballistic missile.

The Strategic Air Command has two Titan missile squadrons deployed near Tucson. Each of the total of 18 weapons is concealed in an underground launching site. All are separated by miles of desert, trained on Soviet targets, armed with nuclear warheads, fuelled and ready to launch. Their purpose is to prevent war.

Each missile has a crew to guard it, care for it and, if need be, fire it. They live underground in a control chamber beside the silo and their whole existence while there is centred around their 'bird.' Living with so much destructive force presents some unique responsibilities for a crew. How seriously they take them, we were soon to see.

The U.S.A.F. had assured us that the weapon and the equipment in the site are so safe that there is practically no chance of an accident. Strict safety rules reduce the risk further. The problem of living with a missile does not lie so much in its potential danger to the crew or surrounding area, but rather in preventing sabotage or its unauthorised firing.

To our right front, about a quarter of a mile from the road, we approached a few small radio masts and a rectangular concrete-coloured structure which hugged the desert floor. Our guide explained that this was the 750-ton sliding door of the silo which we were about to visit.

Our car turned off the road and stopped at the gate of a high wire fence. Two armed airmen came forward and our conducting officer went over to speak to them. He identified himself and one of the sentries, using a portable radio, obtained a clearance for our entry.

The gates were opened and we drove through to halt by a sort of companion-way leading down to a door. By it was a telephone, on which our guide spoke to someone in the control room below the surface. There was the buzz of an electric lock being released, the door opened, and we filed through it down a couple of flights of iron stairs.

There we were halted by another locked door—the one behind us had closed. Surveying us was a closed circuit television camera. The second door opened and, after passing through a further 'blast' door, we found ourselves in the control centre.

The commanding officer, an air force major, greeted us and explained the design of the missile site. Underground were two cylindrical chambers: one of these, the silo proper, contained the missile

9

and was connected by a tunnel to the second, where we were now located.

This had three floors. On the top one were the living quarters, the centre housed the control chamber, and beneath it was a room filled with electronic gear and stores. There were six in the crew, four men underground, and the two guards on the surface. The C.O. invited us to take a gas mask and a safety helmet and go with one of the crew to see the Titan.

We stepped through another door on to an open-work metal platform which ringed the shiny steel bird.

From the bottom of the silo, where the 150-ft. missile rested on springs, nothing linked the weapon to the earth except a small beam of light. Shining into a port in its side, this kept the guidance system oriented with the earth. The nose section was comparatively small— about 10 ft. long—but it contained enough power to destroy a city.

We returned to inspect the living quarters. The metal bunks, linoleum floors and steel walls reminded one of a warship. Our guide opened the refrigerator in the small kitchen and showed us the frozen meals which are provided. Before leaving Tucson for their 24-hour duty shift, the men choose food they would like from the Base kitchen. A large quantity of preserved rations is stored on a lower floor.

Back in the control room the major explained the launching procedure. There were two officers on duty, each of whom had a key. Both of these were needed to initiate the firing system and both officers must have satisfied themselves that the order to fire was genuine before beginning the count-down.

The moment the firing procedure began, a signal light would flash at squadron H.Q., which could stop it by throwing a switch.

As a further precaution against either a madman or accidental firing, no one was allowed to go alone behind the panels containing the wiring of the control system. If one of the guards were to come below ground, he would unload his weapon in front of the television camera before he could enter the control chamber.

The crew did not know the missile's target. The settings to guide the weapon had been worked out at a higher headquarters and meant nothing to the technician who adjusted the guidance system. In theory this would remove some strain from the crew should they have to launch the bird. It might also reduce the possibility of a man developing an animosity toward the target which could tempt him to fire.

We noticed that each of the officers carried a 38 revolver in a holster on his hip. We asked why.

'If you reach for this key which I carry around my neck, I have to shoot you.'

'What if he reaches?' we asked, pointing to the second officer.

'He wouldn't.'

'But supposing he did?'

'He knows that I'd have to shoot him. He'd do the same.'

Deterrence is a personal affair in S.A.C.

An article by Edward Jeffrey in *The Daily Telegraph*

Your Attention Please

The Polar DEW has just warned that
A nuclear rocket strike of
At least one thousand megatons
Has been launched by the enemy
Directly at our major cities.
This announcement will take
Two and a quarter minutes to make,
You therefore have a further
Eight and a quarter minutes
To comply with the shelter
Requirements published in the Civil
Defence Code—section Atomic Attack.
A specially shortened Mass
Will be broadcast at the end
Of this announcement—
Protestant and Jewish services
Will begin simultaneously—
Select your wavelength immediately
According to instructions
In the Defence Code. Do not
Take well-beloved pets (including birds)
Into your shelter—they will consume
Fresh air. Leave the old and bed-
ridden, you can do nothing for them.
Remember to press the ceiling
Switch when everyone is in
The shelter. Set the radiation
Aerial, turn on the geiger barometer.
Turn off your television now.
Turn off your radio immediately
The Services end. At the same time
Secure explosion plugs in the ears
Of each member of your family. Take
Down your plasma flasks. Give your children
The pills marked one and two
In the C.D. green container, then put
Them to bed. Do not break
The inside airlock seals until
The radiation All Clear shows
(Watch for the cuckoo in your
perspex panel), or your District

Touring Doctor rings your bell.
If before this, your air becomes
Exhausted or if any of your family
Is critically injured, administer
The capsules marked 'Valley Forge'
(Red pocket in No. 1 Survival Kit)
For painless death. (Catholics
Will have been instructed by their priests
What to do in this eventuality).
This announcement is ending. Our President
Has already given orders for
Massive retaliation—it will be
Decisive. Some of us may die.
Remember, statistically
It is not likely to be you.
All flags are flying fully dressed
On Government buildings—the sun is shining.
Death is the least we have to fear.
We are all in the hands of God,
Whatever happens happens by His Will.
Now go quickly to your shelters.

                                        Peter Porter

The Second World War. Civilian dead at Dresden.

Conventional Weapons

During the night of February 13th 1945 two heavy bombing raids were carried out by the Royal Air Force upon the German city of Dresden which was almost undefended and packed with refugees. These were followed, the next morning, by a massive American air strike. Here is what Air Marshal Sir Robert Saundby has to say about it:

That the bombing of Dresden was a great tragedy none can deny. That it was a military necessity few . . . will believe. It was one of those terrible things that sometimes happen in wartime, brought about by an unfortunate combination of circumstances. Those who approved it were neither wicked nor cruel, though it may well be that they were too remote from the harsh realities of war to understand fully the appalling destructive power of air bombardment in the spring of 1945.

The advocates of nuclear disarmament seem to believe that, if they could achieve their aim, war would become tolerable and decent. They would do well to . . . ponder the fate of Dresden, where 135,000 people died as the result of an air attack with conventional weapons . . . The atom bomb dropped on Hiroshima killed 71,379 people. (The death roll after the German blitz on Coventry in 1940 was 380.)

Nuclear weapons are, of course, far more powerful nowadays, but it is a mistake to suppose that, if they were abolished, great cities could not be reduced to dust and ashes, and frightful massacres brought about, by aircraft using conventional weapons. And the removal of the fear of nuclear retaliation—which makes modern full-scale war amount to mutual annihilation—might once again make resort to war attractive to an aggressor.

It is not so much this or the other means of making war that is immoral or inhumane. What is immoral is war itself. Once full-scale war has broken out it can never be humanised or civilised, and if one side attempted to do so it would be most likely to be defeated. So long as we resort to war to settle differences between nations, so long will we have to endure the horrors, barbarities and excesses that war brings with it. That, to me, is the lesson of Dresden.

From the foreword to *The Destruction of Dresden* by
David Irving.

2 Censored!

Censors are dead men
set up to judge between life and death.
For no live, sunny man would be a censor,
he'd just laugh!

But censors, being dead men,
have a stern eye on life.
—That thing's alive! It's dangerous. Make away
 with it!—
And when the execution is performed
you hear the stertorous, self-righteous heavy
 breathing of the dead men,
the censors, breathing with relief.

D. H. Lawrence

Is Censorship necessary?

Are you the sort of person who wants to decide absolutely
for himself whether he should attend a play or see a film or
read a book or visit an exhibition *whatever it may be about?*
This question is the first test of your own attitude to censorship. If you answer 'yes' to the whole of it without any
reservation whatsoever, then I would say that you are
against any form of censorship in the arts, that is as far as
you yourself are concerned.

Only a minority of people would have the courage to
answer 'yes' if they were really pressed. When you consider
that without some form of censorship, whether administered
by an official or a policeman is for the moment beside the
point, it would be possible for the arts to portray to the
public, quite indiscriminately, lewdness and blasphemy,
unrestrained vice and perversion, sadism and the cruelties
of the jungle, you will begin to see where censorship quite
naturally begins. The real problem lies in deciding at what
point it should end.

Now this bold minority of people who are prepared to

face anything rather than seek the protection of the police or hide behind a censor, may well draw the line when the same freedom is permitted to other people who they think are weaker-minded than themselves! What is all right for you may not, in your opinion, be all right for your maiden aunt or your fourteen-year-old daughter or your brother-in-law who is a country parson. So you guide them away, or perhaps tell them bluntly they are not to look. And so you will have become a censor yourself.

All this goes to show that there is no easy answer to the censorship problem. Abolish it altogether, and you will soon get an exploitation of public curiosity which will invite some kind of police intervention. Public behaviour over street accidents and murder trials shows there are always plenty of people about who are keen to get a low sort of thrill at any price. It was because of this that censorship began here, and, for that matter, in America.

From *The Film and the Public* by Roger Manvell

Conundrum

Tell me a word
that you've often heard,
yet it makes you squint
if you see it in print!

Tell me a thing
that you've often seen,
yet if put in a book
it makes you turn green!

Tell me a thing
that you often do,
which described in a story
shocks you through and through!

Tell me what's wrong
with words or with you
that you don't mind the thing
yet the name is taboo.

D. H. Lawrence

In Great Britain there is what amounts to a censorship of books, plays and films. Here is how it works:

Books

As long as books were expensive and literacy was confined to a small minority there was little concern over obscene literature. But as public education and cheap books reached the masses, guardians of public morals made their appearance and stimulated governments to suppress obscene writings . . .

The modern law of obscene literature takes as its point of departure Lord Campbell's Act (Obscene Publications Act, 1857). In the Hicklin case (1868) Lord Chief Justice Alexander Cockburn held that the test for obscenity under the statute was 'whether the tendency of the matter charged as obscenity is to deprave and corrupt those whose minds are open to such immoral influences, and into whose hands a publication of this sort may fall.' The test of literary morality was what a father could read aloud in his own home. While there were many successful prosecutions for outright pornography, the law was also invoked against works of literary merit and works with a social or moral purpose. In addition to prosecutions other sanctions were used: seizure of books by the post office, customs officials or police, and their destruction.

The law was subject to continuous attack, for it was widely felt that it often compelled authors to falsify social realities. The law was also attacked for reducing literary standards to the level of what was morally proper for the young. The application of the law by judges in specific cases was also attacked, for judges permitted prosecutions on the basis of isolated passages; and judges also refused to permit evidence of the author's intent or purpose or of his literary reputation, or testimony of recognised literary critics. The law was also attacked because the prosecutions were often directed against booksellers, who were indifferent to the fate of the attacked book.

In some respects these faults in the law or its use no longer obtain. Notable progress was made by Justice

Wintringham Norton Stable in a case before him in Old Bailey (Central Criminal Court, London) in *R* v. *Warburg* (1954). In charging the jury Justice Stable laid down the Hicklin test of obscenity but made a sharp differentiation between 'filth for filth's sake' and literature. The former type of publication has no message, no inspiration, no thought; it is just 'filthy bawdy muck' and such publications are obscene libels. The latter type of publication is one in which the author has 'an honest purpose and an honest thread of thought'; it should not be condemned because it deals with the realities of life, love and sex. He told the jury that sex is not dirty or a sin and that the literary-moral-legal test ought not to be what is suitable for a 14-year-old schoolgirl to read. He also stated his belief that novels are not to be belittled, for they are valuable sources of knowledge about the way people act, feel and think. The jury brought in a verdict of acquittal.

In 1954 an undertaking was initiated in parliament to change Lord Campbell's Act and the effort resulted in enactment of the Obscene Publications Act (1959), the most important provisions of which are: (1) that a person shall not be convicted if publication was 'in the interests of science, literature, art or learning'; (2) that the opinion of experts as to the literary, artistic, scientific or other merits of the publication may be admitted as evidence; (3) that the work is to be read as a whole; and (4) that authors and book publishers may speak in defence of the work though they have not been summoned in the case. In November 1960 a jury in London found that D. H. Lawrence's *Lady Chatterley's Lover* was not obscene.

From *Encyclopaedia Britannica*, 1965

Plays. The situation before 1968

Before a play can be publicly performed in England, it must be read and licensed by the Lord Chamberlain, whose control of the stage derives historically from the functions of the Master of the Revels of Tudor days. Originally this officer was charged with checking riotous behaviour in the theatres and disciplining the actors, who were once legally classified as 'rogues and vagabonds'; he also had power to delete seditious or blasphemous utterances from plays. Gradually his authority was increased, and in Queen Victoria's reign he became a sort of guardian of public morals, with the right to prohibit arbitrarily the performance of any play that offended his sense of propriety. Repeated attempts have been made to abolish this antiquated licensing system, but it is still in full force.

. . . It is said that a licence was almost denied to *The Mikado*, on the ground that it might offend the Imperial Japanese Government. Certain subjects are altogether taboo; thus, for example, for a long time no play that dealt with homosexuality could obtain a licence from the Lord Chamberlain. As is usually the case when an antiquated or absurd law is enforced, means of evasion or violation are easily found. The English device is ridiculously simple. Since the Lord Chamberlain's authority is limited to public performances, the producer organises a 'club' which gives 'private' performances for its 'members'. Membership fees are equivalent to the price of two tickets.

From *The Living Theatre* by Elmer Rice

Censorship by the Lord Chamberlain came to an end in 1968. Since then plays have been subject to possible prosecution for obscenity in the same way as books.

Films

The State takes no part in the censorship of films in Britain, but, by virtue of their power to grant licences, the local licensing authorities act as the final arbiters of films proposed for showing in their areas. There are over 700 licensing authorities: they are local authorities or, in some areas, magistrates. The Cinematograph Act of 1909 required, for reasons of safety, that inflammable films should be shown only on premises licensed for the purpose; it was subsequently established that licensing authorities had the right to supervise the character of the films exhibited. In judging the suitability of films the authorities normally rely on the judgement of an independent body, the British Board of Film Censors, to which are submitted all films (other than newsreels) intended for public showing.

The British Board of Film Censors was set up in 1912 on the initiative of the cinema industry, which wished to ensure that a proper standard was maintained in the films offered to the public. It consists of a president, a secretary, and five examiners (including two women) appointed by the president who is elected by a trade committee and is usually a man prominent in public life.

The Board, which does not use any written code of censorship, may require cuts to be made before it will grant a certificate to a film; very rarely, it will refuse a certificate. Films passed by the Board are placed in one of three categories: 'U' (suitable for universal showing); 'A' (more suitable for adults than children); and 'X' (suitable only for adults). A child or young person under 16 years of age may be admitted to a cinema showing an 'A' film only if accompanied by a responsible adult, and may not be admitted on any condition if an 'X' film is being shown.

From *Britain, An Official Handbook*

Film Censors at work

It is pretty well impossible for a film maker to satisfy all the censors all the time.

In America, for example, sex taboos are still fairly strict but horror and violence are unrestrained. In Sweden the situation is reversed: love scenes are passed happily and in *The Silence* Ingmar Bergman was permitted to show the sexual act (in long shot) but the censor board clamps down heavily on brutality. Both the James Bond films, *Dr. No* and *From Russia with Love*, were subject to several cuts and a number of American films featuring bloody fights have been banned outright. On the other hand, nudist films are allowed even to children 'on the assumption that no child can be harmed mentally by seeing a naked body'.

In France both sex and violence get by but politics are the touchy subject. Indeed, as Peter Graham puts it, the attitude of the *Commission de controle*, 'frequently broadminded towards an exposed nipple or a kick below the belt, has been amply compensated for by a crass hyper-sensitivity to anything of even implied political significance'. We are told that any scene which might compromise France's diplomatic relations with other countries or prejudice her image at home is immediately suppressed. Thus a film version of Maupassant's *Bel Ami,* which referred indirectly to Morocco at the turn of the century, was banned because the dialogue reflected the colonialist attitude of the French at that time. The film was finally cleared in 1956 after all references to Morocco had been removed. When one of the characters asked 'What do the Moroccans think about it?' and was told, 'The Moroccans, Madame, don't think', the word 'Moroccans' was replaced by 'exotic plants'.

Stanley Kubrick's *Paths of Glory* has never been shown publicly in France because it throws an unfavourable light on French military authorities during the 1914-18 war. Renoir's *La Grande Illusion* was banned for making a German officer too sympathetic and Luis Bunuel's *L'Age d'Or* (a film society favourite in England) is still banned thirty-five years after it was made due to the disapproval of the Church.

From an article by Tony Rose in *Amateur Cine World*

The BBC

Sir Hugh Greene, Director-General of the BBC, discusses radio, television and censorship:

The BBC operates under one of the least restricting legal instruments known in Britain, namely a Royal Charter, supported by a licence to operate from the Postmaster-General. These two instruments lay down a relatively small number of things which the BBC must *not* do. It must not carry advertisements or sponsored programmes. It must not express its own opinions about current affairs or matters of public policy. Almost the only positive thing which the Corporation is required to do is to broadcast daily an impartial account of the proceedings of parliament—and even that the BBC started to do on its own initiative, before it was made an obligation. For the rest, the BBC is left to conduct its affairs to the broad satisfaction of the British people (and, in the last analysis, of parliament) under the guidance and legal responsibility of its Governors.

. . . How do we in the BBC interpret and use this freedom? Straight away I should say we do not see this freedom as total licence. We have (and believe strongly in) editorial control. Producers of individual programmes are not simply allowed to do whatever they like. Lines must be drawn somewhere. But, in an operation as diverse in its output as broadcasting, the only sure way of exercising control—here we come to one of my personal beliefs—is to proceed by persuasion and not by written directives; by encouraging the programme staff immediately responsible to apply their judgment to particular problems, within a framework of general guidance arising from the continuing discussion of individual programmes by their seniors—by, that is, the BBC's senior executives and, when necessary, by the Board of Governors. In my view there is nothing to be achieved by coercion or censorship, whether from inside the Corporation or from outside—nothing, that is, except the frustration of creative people who can achieve far more by positive stimulation of their ideas in an atmosphere of freedom.

In stimulating these ideas we have to take account of several important factors, some of which are new to this age of broadcasting, some of which are as old as articulate man himself. We have to resist attempts at censorship. As Professor Richard Hoggart has noted recently, these attempts at censorship come not merely from what he describes as the old 'guardians' (senior clergy, writers of leading articles in newspapers, presidents of national voluntary organisations) who like to think of themselves as upholders of cultural standards although, in many cases, they lack the qualities of intellect and imagination to justify that claim. The attempts at censorship come nowadays also from groups—Hoggart calls them the 'new populists'—which do not claim to be 'guardians' but claim to speak for 'ordinary decent people' and claim to be 'forced to take a stand against' *unnecessary* dirt, *gratuitous* sex, *excessive* violence—and so on. These 'new populists' will attack whatever does not underwrite a set of prior assumptions, assumptions which are anti-intellectual and unimaginative. Superficially this seems like a 'grass-roots' movement. In practice it can threaten a dangerous form of censorship—censorship which works by causing artists and writers not to take risks, not to undertake those adventures of the spirit which must be at the heart of every truly new creative work.

Such a censorship is the more to be condemned when we remember that, historically, the greatest risks have attached to the maintenance of what is right and honourable and true. Honourable men who venture to be different, to move ahead of—or even against—the general trend of public feeling, with sincere conviction and with the intention of enlarging the understanding of our society and its problems, may well feel the scourge of public hostility many times over before their worth is recognised. It is the clear duty of a public-service broadcasting organisation to stand firm against attempts to decry sincerity and vision, whether in the field of public affairs or in the less easily judged world of the arts including the dramatic art.

I believe that broadcasters have a duty not to be diverted by arguments in favour of what is, in fact, disguised censorship. I believe we have a duty to take account of the changes in society, to be ahead of public opinion rather than always to wait upon it. I believe that great broadcasting organisations, with their immense powers of patronage for writers and artists, should not neglect to cultivate young writers who may, by many, be considered 'too advanced,' even 'shocking'. Such allegations have been made throughout the ages. Many writers have been condemned as subversive when first published. Henrik Ibsen, for example, was at

23

c

one time regarded as too shocking for his plays to be staged in Britain. At least in the secular and scientific fields, today's heresies often prove to be tomorrow's dogmas. And, in the case of the potential Ibsens of today, we must not, by covert censorship, run the risk of stifling talents which may prove great before they are grown.

I do not need to be reminded that broadcasting has access to every home, and to an audience of all ages and varying degrees of sophistication. We must rely, therefore, not only on our own disciplines but on those which have to be exercised by, among others, parents. Programme plans must, to my mind, be made on the assumption that the audience is capable of reasonable behaviour, and of the exercise of intelligence—and of choice. No other basis will meet the needs of the situation. How *can* one consciously plan for the unreasonable or the unintelligent? It is impossible, or if not strictly speaking impossible, utterly disastrous.

Editorial discretion must concern itself with two aspects of the content of broadcasting—subjects and treatments. If the audience is to be considered as it really is—as a series of individual minds (each with its own claim to enlightenment, each of different capacity and interests) and not as that statistical abstraction the *'mass'* audience—then it would seem to me that no subject can be excluded from the range of broadcasting simply for being what it is. The questions which we must face are those of identifying the times and the circumstances in which we may expect to find the intended audience for a given programme.

Relevance is the key—relevance to the audience, and to the tide of opinion in society. Outrage is wrong. Shock may not be good. Provocation can be healthy and indeed socially imperative. These are the issues to which the broadcaster must apply his conscience. But treatment of the subject, once chosen, demands the most careful assessment of the reasonable limits of tolerance in the audience, if there is any likelihood of these limits being tested by the manner of presentation of the material. As I have said, however, no subject is (for me) excluded simply for what it is.

24 From an article in *The Listener*

The real reasons behind censorship?

Censorship comes into play when those who dominate our systems of social control begin to feel a threat either to their power or to the system which has been long accepted. Actually, of course, those who are the operating agents of social control—formal or informal—usually identify the preservation of traditional controls with their own status and power. Among other areas of thought and conduct which have experienced the threat or actuality of censorship in our society are discussions of biological evolution and its implications for morals and religion, critiques of the Bible and Christian writings which put them in an adequate historical and psychological perspective, attacks on the political and economic order by revolutionaries, and, perhaps most common of all, the treatment of sex. These clearly represent basic values in our culture.

Instances of censorship both in peacetime and in war are ample. Books like *Lady Chatterley's Lover*, *Strange Fruit*, and even classics like *The Decameron* have come under the ban in various communities . . . With respect to the educational programmes designed for men in military services, there have been periodic attempts to prevent alleged subversive materials from reaching them. The lengths to which military officialdom may go is illustrated in a case where a book of readings for general economics was banned because one reprinted piece therein was a selection from *The Communist Manifesto* by Marx and Engels.

To ask why such books, either in the political or literary field, should be attacked raises questions both at the institutional and the psychological level of interpretation. Regarding the institutional analysis, there is no doubt that some persons and some organised groups in this country *(the U.S.A.)* feel threatened by criticism of their deep-seated convictions on politics, economics, and morals. They easily make use of the generally unsettled psychological atmosphere of wartime to take legal or other measures to ban certain publications. The camouflage of crying 'Wolf, Wolf' is an old one, and many people may quickly associate the call for censorship with the preservation of values which really have little to do with the issue. Thus, it is easier to attack *The Grapes of Wrath* as a nasty book than to examine the basic causes of population mobility under conditions of drought and hard times, or to expose the exploitation of farm labour under the highly commercialised agriculture of some sections of our country. It reminds one of the familiar tendency to blame the motion pictures for much of our juvenile delinquency rather than to spend time in seeking out and curing the more direct causes of personal demoralisation in our urban society.

Censorship always reveals our deep moral values in the face of changes. So, too, it reveals in our local and national life the persistence of certain agencies who consider themselves the keepers of the moral ideas and the moral conduct of others. There is no doubt that certain class standards, certain political views, and many traditional codes regarding sex are still protected by powerful interests that do not wish to see them altered. Among such agencies which support tradition are conservative churches, especially those long accustomed to controlling the reading and thinking of their congregations. Then, too, there are the lingering followers of Anthony Comstock *(a leading American crusader against what he regarded as the immoral publications of his day. He died in* 1915) who still find considerable community support for their periodical forays against any printed matter which they consider to be obscene, pornographic and contrary to public decency. These do-gooders often rationalise or excuse their suppression of a free press and free speech in terms which carry a lot of emotional freight and appear to represent values of utmost importance to the continuity of our society. It is an appeal which is bound to find much support, since it symbolises at least one area in which some stability, some link with tradition and custom, may be found in these otherwise troublesome and changing times.

From *Handbook of Social Psychology* by Kimball Young

3 In trouble with the police

Why do young people get into trouble with the police? A variety of reasons are suggested in the following passages.

Planned fire 'to repay teacher'

A 13-YEARS-OLD boy admitted at Radstock juvenile court yesterday that he set fire to hay and a shed at a school.

He was placed on probation for three years and his father was ordered to pay £15 compensation and 15s. court fees.

It was stated that the boy had planned the fire as a means of repaying one of the masters who had admonished him.

From the *Bath Evening Chronicle*

Incendiary

That one small boy with a face like pallid cheese
And burnt-out little eyes could make a blaze
As brazen, fierce and huge, as red and gold
And zany yellow as the one that spoiled
Three thousand guineas' worth of property
And crops at Goodwin's Farm on Saturday
Is frightening, as fact and metaphor:
An ordinary match intended for
The lighting of a pipe or kitchen fire
Misused may set a whole menagerie
Of flame-fanged tigers roaring hungrily.
And frightening, too, that one small boy should set
The sky on fire and choke the stars to heat
Such skinny limbs and such a little heart
Which would have been content with one warm kiss,
Had there been anyone to offer this.

Vernon Scannell

A young offender

Here is part of a conversation between Wilfrid De'Ath, a BBC talks producer, and a young man of nineteen who is now 'going straight' and studying at a technical college.

I came from a home which was from the age of about eleven divided into two. There was my father; he was in the Navy from the time I was born right up to the age of about four or five. I saw him very little; and I saw him very little when I was about six, seven, or eight because he was working, and he used to travel up to London during the week. I can't remember my mother and father quarrelling, but there was a sort of distinct break.
Were you aware of this at such an early age?
I think really I was aware of it from about eleven onwards when I first started having my own ideas, wanting to do what

I wanted rather than what my father wanted. I remember the very first quarrel I had. I got into trouble with the police. I was with a few friends, and we went into a field and started breaking down a sort of little hut. We would play on it and generally pull it to pieces, quite harmlessly. All my friends would do this; and one day I went over there for the very first time, and I was pulling bits of wood off when suddenly from out of nowhere came a farmer carrying a shotgun. He had a dog with him, and one of his assistants. They grabbed the three of us and bundled us into a car and took us off down to the nearest police station, and we were charged. My father went up to see the farmer that night, after he had heard about it, and tried to get him to withdraw the charge. They all went down to the police station, and they said 'well we're terribly sorry but we can't', and I had to go to court about a week later.

How old were you then?

I was eleven. My father was very upset. This was just at the time he persuaded me to pass my eleven-plus, and offered me £8—which he retracted when I got into trouble. I still passed the eleven-plus, but from then onwards I've always found it difficult to communicate with my father. I don't think he has ever forgiven me for that first incident.

Can you explain to yourself now the basis for the difference between you and your father? What is it?

He was very intelligent and he was brought up in a very hard way. His father died quite early, and he was pushed into the Navy instead of going to college. Having been in the Navy for so long and having come from a background where mother is the main influence, he is very, very rigid and authoritative; and he bases such ridiculous arguments on my behaviour, things about manners, politeness, haircuts, instead of important things.

Do you see him now?

No, I haven't seen him for four years, since I left home. I've bumped into him a couple of times; I bumped into him six months ago. I was at my mother's place having a meal during the day, and he came in and ordered me out of the house straight away, which upset me. Even after I passed my examination at school, and I left home, and eventually after getting into trouble I managed to do fairly well and get an education, go to evening classes, that sort of thing, he still built up this resentment against me. He's got the idea that I'm permanently doomed to be a criminal or something. I think it is a case of me not being what he wants me to be.

Do you hope ever to get on good terms with him again?

It may be better when I am twenty-four, twenty-five; perhaps I'll be able to go back and see him and speak to him much more sensibly, without any emotional outbursts, but it is completely impossible at the moment.

What about your mother?

My mother is somehow the complete opposite of my father: she is very well balanced, a complete sort of working-class housewife. She never worries about anything for very long; she's a very good mother and a very good wife. I suppose that is the reason I get on with her; she doesn't tell me what to do very much, although we have arguments.

Why wasn't your mother sufficient to keep you respectable?

I think it needed the authority, or at least the friendship, of a father for me to come through without getting into trouble; but I had no sort of guiding hand from my father after the age of eleven.

We have agreed that you felt alienated from that age. Was this a very conscious feeling? Did you feel, at the age of eleven or twelve, 'I am different from other boys'?

I did. I can remember isolated incidents, especially when I was fourteen or fifteen, at grammar school, when I felt completely different from everybody else. I had three or four very close friends in grammar school, and I was too embarrassed to bring them home. I had a girl-friend who was fifteen, and I was just under fifteen, and she sent me a postcard one day when she went on holiday. I was looking forward to getting this, but before I got it my father rushed down and picked it up from the doormat and started reading it, and started making fun of me for the sort of language she was using on the postcard, which was obviously pretty crazy. The worst thing I think really was my father and me and haircuts. Every three weeks I would be sitting at the breakfast table just before going to school, and he'd rush up behind me and poke his finger in my neck and say: 'Have a haircut tonight, here's the three shillings'; and I used not to come home that night until quite late and sneak into my bedroom to avoid getting a haircut. It got to the stage where I would go to the barber's and have a haircut as long as possible within the regions of 'short back and sides', and my father would take me back the day after and I would be sitting in the barber's chair feeling terrible, with the barber clipping away with the shears and my father telling him to cut it shorter. We never quarrelled about really big things, it was just these small things like table manners, the correct way to eat with a knife and fork or to pick up a cup of tea, which to me didn't matter one damn.

If you can point to a moment in time, when did the break come with your family?

Strangely enough it was the final row about haircuts. I was supposed to be in by nine o'clock when I was fifteen. I came home at half past nine—I'd been over to see some friends—and I had the biggest row with my father that I'd ever had. He said: 'Well I don't want you in the house, get out'; and I got out. I went back to see if my friends were up, but their doors were locked; they'd gone to bed, and I just wandered around the streets. I wandered round by the river, and sat on a park bench and tried to go to sleep. I was woken up at about two in the morning by a policeman who took me down to the station, and phoned up my parents. I went back home, and the day after I left, and went into a sort of hostel for six months until I passed my G.C.E. exams at grammar school. Then I left and I got a flat. One of the jobs I had, I was working in a library, and I was standing there taking books in, and I accidentally opened a book and I found a cheque in it, and I went along to a Co-op store and cashed the cheque. I still don't know how I managed to do it because it was £20, and I looked pretty dirty and ragged. I went out and spent it; and about a week later the police called round at my house and said: 'You know what we've come for'. I sort of stood there shaking, and they dragged me down to the police station. I was there most of the night, and I got charged and taken to a magistrate's court, and I was given two years' probation.

Were you conscious of doing something wrong?

No, I don't think I was at the time. I very badly needed money. I was earning about £6 a week and I was paying £2 10s. a week rent for my room, and I was thinking very short term. There was a complete absence of guilt, as a matter of fact. That evening I walked into a coffee bar, where I usually went. I bought lots of meals and drinks for everybody; people were saying 'Where did you get the money from? You must have pinched it', and I said 'Well of course, I'm good at doing things like that', and it didn't matter to them. We went out, and, although I wanted clothes very badly and I wanted some books, I spent most of it on drink and getting into various clubs and that sort of thing.

How did you react to being put on probation? Was it a shock to your system, did it pull you up in any way?

No. I resented the idea of having to go to see a probation officer once every two or three weeks, but apart from that it didn't make any difference at all to me.

What was the probation officer like?

I had two. They were both very good. I talked about all sorts of things to them. They never told me what to do; I didn't have to report to them very regularly after the first six months, and they were quite interested to know how I was getting on. They certainly didn't interfere with me.

Did you have any dealings at that time—about the age of sixteen, seventeen—with anyone else who was on probation, or anyone who was in trouble with the law?

Well at the sort of coffee bars that I went to, the jazz clubs that I went to, everybody had at some time or another brushed with the law.

Is there any glamour in this for you?

Tremendous amount of glamour, not so much for theft or for breaking and entering, but for drug addiction. I had a friend who was working in a big firm that produced benzedrine, and he'd go into the production line and chat up a couple of the girls and come away with 1,000 of these pills every week. He'd take them over to the jazz club and sell them. We'd take three or four of these capsules of benzedrine on a Friday night, and hang around the area, just walking about the streets and talking like mad and jumping all over the place. We wouldn't sleep at all on Friday nights. On Saturday we'd be in the same area; then we'd go to the jazz club on Saturday night, and much later on Saturday night we'd go up into London on the train, and go to Collier's Jazz Club—the all-night session—and stay there until Sunday morning, and wander around Soho on Sunday morning and walk back all the way along the river, back to the place where we came from.

Did you take any other drugs apart from benzedrine?

I'd had marijuana a couple of times. There were a few of my friends who'd take nothing else but marijuana; the main drug that I took was benzedrine. I suppose in a sense I was addicted to it, although it's not normally physically addictive. At weekends I'd take probably eight of these capsules, which would keep me awake for two nights, and of course the next two days at work—Monday and Tuesday—were pretty horrible, and by the time Wednesday came I was looking forward to the weekend.

What was the kick, I mean particularly? Just to be kept awake, to feel good for two days?

Yes, you get a tremendous amount of energy from it, and you're talking all the time, incessantly, you think you're a genius. I think one of the best things is that you're walking around all the time in the streets at night, and it's pouring down with rain, you haven't got a coat on, and you just can't stop walking—you run everywhere.

Was there a definite group of you who used to do this every weekend, boys and girls?

Yes, yes; I suppose thirty people, with odd people sort of coming here and there from other places, coming into the town for six months, staying there and being part of the set, and then just going off. Everybody did that.

We were talking about the kind of definite formal brushes with authority: we had first of all the time you smashed up a hut, then the time you cashed a cheque for £20. What was the next one would you say—the big one?

The next one was the big one, although the offence wasn't really very serious, I suppose. I was working in a wine and spirit merchants just before Christmas, and everybody would knock off half a bottle of whisky, quarter bottle of whisky, every day and take it home. Of course I did the same thing. I was going to rather a lot of parties at that stage, and I liked drinking, so I'd just take these things.

How much did you take?

I'd take about a quarter bottle a day. I was bottling the stuff, so I'd just get any small bottle from the shelf and fill it up and put it in my pocket and walk out in the evenings.

Over how long a period of time were you doing this?

This was only three weeks, because I was caught after I was working there for three weeks. I'd take this stuff back to my room and keep it in a cupboard, and at the time I was living with rather an old, Victorian-type landlady who didn't really like me but wanted the money, and I had a girl-friend to stay fairly regularly. One weekend she stayed, and the landlady found out, and a couple of days later I went in to work and suddenly the police came and took me off down to the station. They said 'We know you've been pinching this stuff, so if you tell us all about it then everything will be okay and you'll probably get a fine because everybody does this'. Apparently my landlady had searched my room and read all my letters from previous friends, went all through my stuff and found this whisky, and she knew that I was working at this wine and spirits merchants, and she must have thought I pinched it, so she phoned them up.

When you were pinching the whisky, was the fact that you were on probation on your mind? Or were you off probation?

No. It was getting near the time to finish, and I remember this is the thing that shocked me most. I'd just been caught, and I was walking back to my flat with a couple of policemen because they wanted to search it, and suddenly I realised 'Oh Christ, I'm on probation, I've had it'.

So you wouldn't have done it if you'd remembered that you'd been on probation. Is that what you're trying to say?

It wasn't a case of forgetting that I was on probation, you know, it just wasn't in my mind at the time; I didn't think. You see it was so natural to do because I was surrounded by bottles of wine, bottles of whisky, everything you can imagine; and everybody was taking the stuff. Friends of mine had got away with—oh whole lorry-loads of the stuff. Poor me, taking a couple of bottles of whisky, I'd had it.

What was your feeling about being picked up?

I think in all these things there are two traumatic experiences, the first one is being picked up and the second one is being charged; and I felt completely horrible. This was the end for me because I knew I was going to get into big trouble because I was on probation. It happened so quickly; I was, I suppose, conned by police methods into telling them everything, and thinking about it now I probably could have gotten away with a fine, a fairly small fine, because everybody was doing it. But they got all the details about what I'd been doing, how I did it, and I think they decided to make an example of me. I was given three months' detention.

Would you have been given a sentence like that if you hadn't been on probation already?

I'm not sure, because it was Monday morning, and the magistrate certainly looked a bastard even if he wasn't. Strangely enough, two days after I'd been caught, some other friends of mine had been caught for exactly the same offence and they were sent to the same place as me, and it finally got to the point where they'd had to stop this at all costs and make it public, and so they gave me three months.

What was the detention centre like?

Pretty horrible. The idea behind a detention centre is that you're given a short, sharp shock. It's the last stage before going to Borstal or prison, and the routine is rather like being in the army; you're rushing around all the time, marching and doing work, clearing snow off the roads, chopping wood, rushing up and down doing physical training every day from about six in the morning until nine at night.

Was this a terrible shock to you personally, a place like this?

It was a complete shock. I didn't realise how quickly your whole conception of yourself, your whole identity could be broken down. You'd go in there, and on the first day you'd see these people at meal-times eating like complete pigs, grabbing food off their plate and shovelling it into their mouths and eating the very last crust, and you think 'Christ, I can't be like that'; and you find that in two weeks' time you're exactly like it.

So the short, sharp, shock stuff, does it work?

I don't know whether it worked with me or not. I haven't

been in trouble with the police since, but on the other hand I know lots of people who were in there at the same time as me have been in trouble; and the success rates have been published, and it is about 30 to 40 per cent successful with most people. The main thing it does, I think, is to reinforce your attitude towards authority; because your attitude is quite strong: it's always 'Them' and 'Us', you know, like in *The Loneliness of the Long Distance Runner;* and you're just you running your own separate race, and you don't care what anybody does. The first thing you want to do is to get out and live your own life, but you come up feeling they're all bastards, they hate me.

There were two types of officers—warders—there. The worst type was the young ones, just about twenty-five. They were very petty, very childish, and very very unpleasant. They'd make you do all sorts of ridiculous things, like doing press-ups in the snow for talking out of place. And the other type, they were quite good. There was one—he'd been working at Dartmoor most of his life—and he was quite friendly; you could talk to him, and he thought the whole idea of detention centres was a load of nonsense. He was very sympathetic towards most of us.

Did they do anything that you would say was unfair?

It depends whether you regard clearing snow off the roads at eight in the morning with a pick-axe, wearing only overalls, as unfair.

What else did they do that you would condemn?

Getting up at six in the morning, rushing into the canteen to drink half a mug of cold cocoa, and then going on to the parade ground to do press-ups and jumping up and down in the snow, and then coming in, getting washed . . .

Did they beat up anyone, these people?

Just as I came in, some people were in the punishment cells. They'd escaped a couple of weeks earlier. The technique is that they get you into these punishment cells and then three or four of them will come down. They'll strip you and they'll beat you up very carefully, or they'll take you over to the gymnasium and roll you in a mat and kick you, so that there are no bad bruises or anything like that; or they'll just pass the word round amongst themselves that

37

everybody is to take it out on you, so that anything the whole camp does, you do twice as much.

Did they ever beat you up?

They never beat me up, no; I managed to avoid it. I was very quiet and careful, apart from one or two odd times. I was the cigarette baron. It was rather funny because I was sort of trusted because obviously I was fairly intelligent, and I used to go out on the outside of the camp and clear snow off the roads, and I used to chat up the Governor's son, and he'd drop a packet of cigarettes and I'd hide them down my trousers and come in and sell them at night for bits of bread. This was the main thing in this place—food.

Did you feel that in any sense the others deserved to be there and that you didn't?

No, you never think about this when you're inside a place like that. You accept the fact that some people commit crimes, they knock cars off, they beat people up, or they break into houses. It's just their way of life; but you've got no sense of guilt. This is probably the whole thing which is wrong with any punishment like that: it's completely retributive and it doesn't alter your ideas so that you feel you have done something socially wrong.

How did it feel when you came out?

Marvellous. I came out about, oh, seven in the morning one day. It was a Monday morning, and this place was in completely flat countryside with just odd trees and stunted bushes, and I had to walk for about two miles to the station. I rushed out of the gates and just started running anywhere —just like that; and I bought a packet of cigarettes because you weren't allowed to smoke in there. I hadn't smoked for three months, and it was really marvellous. You go to a kiosk: 'Twenty cigarettes, please'.

In your opinion, as far as you can give it, this short, sharp shock business doesn't work?

I don't think it does, no. The main thing it does is to reinforce your attitude. It doesn't teach you to think, it doesn't stop you committing crimes.

What did you do when you came out?

The first thing I did was to go to the Labour Exchange and get some money, because they owed me some. I went to the tax office and got some money, and I went to a friend of mine and asked if he could put me up. I stayed there for six months. I came out in February, and in summer I was due to take my 'A' level examinations, so I decided the best thing to do would be to stay on the dole for six months, and try and study to get these examinations and then go to college, or go to work, depending on the results.

From *The Listener*

A professional criminal

'The Courage of His Convictions' is the story of a professional criminal who has spent $12\frac{1}{2}$ of his 33 years in prison. His crimes have included theft, housebreaking, safe blowing, armed robbery, robbery with violence, assault on the police and causing grievous bodily harm.

The funny thing is, my father was straight. Sometimes I think if he hadn't been I mightn't have taken to crime. But I'm only guessing. Probably it wouldn't have made any difference at all.

My grandfather was a pickpocket, my six uncles were all villains and tearaways, my brothers and friends were thieves, and most of the neighbours were in and out of prison like pigeons in a loft. So for a long time, in fact, my father was the only straight man I knew.

He was good and kind and honest—but, as I saw it as a kid, all it got him was poverty. He was a socialist—almost a communist—and he was always talking about changing the system which brought richness to some and poverty to many. He believed it could be done by education and political activity, by arguing and getting people round to his point of view. I was too impatient for that. I believed the system was wrong, too, but I knew it wouldn't ever be changed by our sort. I didn't want to wait two hundred years for the day when everyone had fair shares. I wanted to take part in the levelling-up of wealth myself, and make sure *I* got some benefit from it. And I wanted to start

D

getting on with it there and then.

. . . Naturally I had to spend part of my life at school, but it was as little as I could make it, because I didn't like it. Subjects like history and geography were all right, and I enjoyed running and boxing and other sports. But the big trouble was school meant obedience to authority, and this is something I've never taken to. They tried to get this into me more than any subject on the curriculum, but it didn't work. Punishments made no difference, whatever sort they were, beatings or anything else.

. . . There were times I was whacked so hard I could feel the weals on my arse like corrugated cardboard. One woman teacher gave it me for throwing a board-duster, and her system was that you had to say, in between each stroke: 'I will not throw board-dusters,' or whatever you'd done. I wouldn't say it, so she kept hitting harder each time to try and make me, but I still wouldn't. Exasperated, she grabbed at my belt and tried to pull my pants down so she could beat me on my bare flesh. To do that, she had to put the cane down, and I picked it up and slashed at her with it until her screaming brought one of the masters running in.

The punishment the headmaster decided on for that was twenty-four stripes laid on in front of the whole school. At least he didn't try to take my trousers off, so I just gritted my teeth and thought damn them all, and eventually it was over.

Afterwards I went out into the bicycle shed, found the bike of the woman teacher and slashed her tyres to ribbons, and then I went back inside to the cloakroom with a lump of old iron I'd found and smashed up the sinks.

That was how I felt then, and I've not changed much. When someone acts primitively towards you, you act primitively back, on the same level as you're treated. Attempting to destroy something that is part of me—however unpleasant or reprehensible a characteristic it is—only makes me want to destroy something of authority's in return.

I should think the product I am today ought to prove thrashings are no good, and only produce responses of vengeance and violence. It makes me laugh when I read of the Tory women at Bournemouth calling for a return of the cat. Even on what you might call simply an economic basis, I and all the people I know would prefer the cat to a long sentence any time. After three days it doesn't hurt any more, and the scars soon heal, except those on your mind. What you feel is anger, resentment, and, most of all, a determination somehow to get your own back. But being deterred? The idea never gets a look in.

The only thing that gets anywhere at all is kindness. It might not get far, but it's got much more chance than anything else. I'd like to make it clear, though, that this isn't an appeal for kindness in dealing with criminals. I think kindness is probably better for the people who are handing it out, but that's all. As a criminal myself, it's a matter of indifference to me whether I'm treated kindly or cruelly, and neither will change me. For others—well, with kindness there is always the faint hope they might respond: but anyone who responds to ill-treatment and brutality must be solid from the neck up.

. . . I don't believe you can defend the use of violence at all, in any circumstances. It's wrong whoever uses it and whatever they use it for. It's wrong when I use it, it's wrong when American maniacs drop an atom-bomb on Hiroshima or Nagasaki, when the South African police shoot down Africans at Sharpeville, when a man commits murder, when 'respectable' society takes him and hangs him as punishment, when Eden orders the British Air Force to bomb Port Said. This is all wrong, every time.

You get this in Parliament a lot, these politicians, usually the Tories, who start screaming off about the increase in crimes of violence, and how 'these thugs have got to be stopped'—these same fellers who were waving their order-papers and dancing up and down with delight when they thought we'd bombed the 'Egyptian wogs' into submission. Who are they to tell me that I'm beyond the pale for using violence?

. . . It just happens that it's a tool of my trade and I use it—like an engineer uses a slide-rule, or a bus-driver the handbrake, or a dentist the drill. Only when necessary, and only when it can't be avoided. If I've got to whack a bloke with an iron bar to make him let go of a wages-bag he's carrying, O.K., so I'll whack him. If he lets go without any trouble, I don't. That's all.

. . . Violence is in a way like bad language—something that a person like me's been brought up with, something I got used to very early on as part of the daily scene of childhood, you might say. I don't at all recoil from the idea, I don't have a sort of inborn dislike of the thing, like you do. As long as I can remember I've seen violence in use all around me—my mother hitting the children; my brothers and sisters all whacking one another, or other children; the man downstairs bashing his wife, and so on. You get used to it, it doesn't mean anything in these circumstances.

. . . If I go after a bloke to give him a stripe for something, it's more than likely that if I do stripe him not long afterwards he'll come looking for me, trying to do the same thing back again. I don't object to this, in fact I expect him to do it: I know I'd do the same myself if it was the other way round.

But I think when the police use it for instance—which they quite often do—when they're trying to pin something on you and haven't got enough evidence unless they can get you to confess—well, this I think is wrong. They're supposed to be upholding the Law, not taking it into their own hands. Mind you, an odd beating from the police is just another occupational hazard, so one's got to put up with it, but all the same it doesn't make me respect them any more. They think I'm just a beetle-browed mental defective, but I've got my standards—and I don't go in for beating up people with a gang of my mates, all of us on to him in one room, like they do. I'll fight anyone any fashion he likes, fair fight or foul fight, and, like I said, if he comes off worst I'm not surprised if he comes after me again later, trying to even the score. But when the police give you a beating you can't go and do them up afterwards: you've just got to take it, and from the very people who are supposed to be getting you to lay off violence as a method.

From *The Courage of His Convictions*
by Robert Allerton as told to Tony Parker

A sociologist's explanation

It is not unusual for a disturbed child, or even a grown-up, to steal almost worthless objects, and then to hide them away in an attic, or under a carpet as if the thought that they were there was in itself a source of comfort to him.

Such a person was Dennis, a deprived child who had just left school and before taking a job on a farm was training for his future work in a hostel. The other boys in the hostel complained that their property was being stolen and eventually traced the thefts to Dennis. Without his knowledge they watched through the dining-room window as he opened up a hole behind the garage in the hostel garden, and took out an old raincoat. Inside was wrapped a motley collection of articles: money, a watch, a penknife, handkerchiefs, a diary —all the items of personal property which had disappeared over the previous fortnight. As he surveyed his hoard he looked happier than he ever was in his normal life about the hostel. Discussion with him confirmed how much reassurance he gained from having this secret treasure. To possess momentarily seems often to provide transient feelings of being loved to the deprived, but to have one's booty thus permanently available, to be handled and gloated over, seems to provide a kind of permanent reservoir of love, a kind of mother-substitute. But Dennis's mother-substitute in the hole behind the garage could never provide him with real love, and by thus assuaging his feelings of insecurity, enable him to grow out of dependence on her in the way that the normal child grows out of his dependence upon his mother.

An additional unconscious motive is often to be discerned. A child who steals may be not only stealing gratifications (such as sweets or money) by which he seeks to compensate himself for his lack of love, but may also be expressing his resentment at having been deprived in this way. The formula seems to be 'You haven't given me love as you should have done; therefore I am going to take it and so get my own back.'

One of the commonest results of the frustrations which training necessarily imposes is such anger. Both in the psychological laboratory and in the psychiatric clinic it is found that, although other ways of meeting frustration are possible, the commonest way in early childhood is likely to be with intense anger. As the frustrators are most likely to be a child's parents, and in particular his mother, who are essential to his physical survival and the main sources to which he must look for love, the direct expression of aggression towards them is bound to be inhibited. To be angry with one's mother is seen by the ego as dangerous, or even later on by the moral sense (the superego) as wicked and the angry feelings are therefore repressed. Because they are unconscious and unexpressed, they continue unabated, and if frustrations are excessive, then the individual becomes an 'angry person', seeking a target for his anger outside the family. There are many such ways of expressing intense hostility, but one way is through violent crime.

This may consist of the wanton destruction of property, or of assault, or even murder. In some cases, where the anger is a result of the frustration suffered by the young child in his relationship with authority figures in his family (often, in European society, his father), the aggressiveness thus evoked in him may be deflected upon authority in general. Anti-authority attitudes of this kind may lead to nonconformity in religion, politics, or convention; but sometimes they lead an individual into a bitter and unremitting war against other paternal surrogates like the law and the police. Such a person can be a very dangerous and incorrigible type of criminal.

All of this, of course, is going on under the surface and people will often argue that such explanations are merely an attempt to find an excuse for a scoundrel, whose acts are much more easily explained as the result of avarice or vice. No one is likely to jump at such a suggestion more readily than the criminal himself. He will be glad to accept convincing rationalisations for his behaviour. The real explanation has already been found intolerable, and although the individual may have progressed a good deal in maturity since then, the earlier association would still be strong enough to deter him from digging it up again. Tied up with rationalisation is the use of symbols to disguise our real objectives. Apparently innocuous acts or things have significance in our unconscious lives, 'standing for' some repressed wish, and facilitating a comfortable rationalisation about it. Thus articles stolen, as in the earlier discussion, may be said to be symbols for gratification and, therefore, love, but can also plausibly be seen as objects which are wanted for their own sake.

. . . If in the grossly deprived, the superego (moral sense) is weak, in others, as acquired in infancy, it is often itself a major obstacle to the personal development of the individual. It is, after all, not based upon the child's own individual evaluations, but upon the assumption of a set of values, taken at second-hand from someone else. Nor are these, often, very accurate, even as copies. We are all very apt to understand other people's emotions and motivations in the light of our own. We can have no direct experience of what is going on in their minds, and so, for example, must interpret a statement by someone else that he is 'happy' as meaning that he feels as we feel when we are happy. To project our own states of mind upon other people in this way is not necessarily misleading, but may be so if our own state of mind is very different from theirs. The state of mind of a young child is very different from that of his parents: he is very vulnerable emotionally, and only too easily projects his own strong feelings and wishes upon his parents. Thus he is apt to perceive parental prohibitions as much stronger than they are, and as a result to acquire a superego which is more censorious than ever his parents were. If his upbringing has been highly moralistic, the result, when this has been magnified into the infantile superego, may be to prohibit so many satisfactions as to gravely impoverish his personality and his life.

We all know people like this, living very narrowly circumscribed lives, to whom almost anything enjoyable is 'wicked'. This must not only reduce their own pleasure in living, and the contribution they can make to life, but also means that their inner lives are a constant battleground between instinctual wishes, and an ego acting under the lash of a puritanical moral judgement, to keep them in check. It is out of such acute inner conflict that neurosis arises, or alternatively unconsciously motivated criminality as another kind of neurotic symptom. The psychiatrist's objective in treatment must then become such a degree of self-knowledge on the part of the individual as will enable him to temper the severity of this despotic conscience of his. One of the signs of the mature person is that he has begun gradually to replace the irrational and second-hand moral judgements embodied in the infantile superego by a more realistic morality based upon ideas of right and wrong which he has evolved for himself out of his own experience. And this implies, also, that moral choices are brought out into the light instead of emerging, full-grown and unchallengeable, out of an unconscious mental process.

This view of human psychological development is built four-square on Freud's basic assumption of 'psychic determinism'. Personality, and even personal morality, are seen as the result of a process of development over which the individual has little or no control. The highly moral person is not so because of any particular virtue on his part, but because of the accidents of his early years; and instead of admiring him, we may often have reason to pity him as someone whose early training has taken away from him much of the capacity for the enjoyment of life.

The case of Fred Brown shows how irrational an unconsciously nurtured sense of guilt may be, leading even to criminality rather than to its opposite. He went into a tobacconist's to buy cigarettes, and when the old lady behind the counter recognised him and began to scream, he hesitated too long and was seized. Only a week before, it appeared, Fred had held her up in the street and robbed her of her purse. Now here he was, brazenly undisguised (or as she seemed to be saying, disguised as an honest man) in her shop.

Such behaviour on his part sounds very stupid, and yet Fred is anything but stupid. It was not a question at all of his being unable to understand; but he seems to be driven by something within himself which he cannot control. He has to go on committing crimes, and always seems somehow to place himself in such a position that he will afterwards be caught. Most of the last thirty years of his life have been spent in prison. He tries to explain it all away—mainly, it seems, to satisfy his own inner questionings about his way of life. So he talks about easy money, and not having to work, but he knows inside himself that his life is empty and aimless, and that he spends it either in poverty outside prison, or in privation and hard labour inside.

What has become known about his history throws a little light upon his problems. Fred as a child received little love from his parents. Then a baby brother arrived on the scene. All normal children are apt in these circumstances to be jealous of the new arrival, but because Fred felt so insecure already his resentment was extreme. His mother and father doted on the new arrival, and even called on little Fred to agree with them, saying, 'Isn't he a darling, Fred? Such a cute little thing, and so pretty'. Fred always smiled, but inside he was intensely jealous. His violent daydreams about the baby frightened him, and had to be obliterated. When they had been, he was able to be kind to his little rival, even though jealous feelings still persisted on the fringes of his mind.

Then a catastrophe occurred: the baby was accidentally smothered by the blankets covering his cot. To Fred, his death must have seemed like the enactment of his own unconscious wishes against his brother. He had never committed any act of overt hostility against the baby, but in the unconscious the desire to do so is enough. Fred has carried with him an unconscious burden of guilt ever since. Like the rest of us, he seeks assuagement of his guilt through punishment, but he commits crimes in order that he may be punished for an act which he has committed only in his own mind. This means that his guilty feelings are hardly likely to be relieved, no matter how much punishment he receives, for he is caught in a vicious circle, seeking punishment again and again, but never managing to cancel out more than his sense of responsibility for his current delinquencies. By comparison with the enormity of the crime which obsesses him, these, both delinquencies and punishments alike, are trivial. And the sense of guilt remains unconscious; all *he* knows is that he must go on offending against the law, and that somehow he always manages to get himself caught.

The conventional and common-sense way of dealing with misbehaviour is by means of deterrent punishment, but in a case like that of Fred where a criminal actually seeks punishment, it is no deterrent, but an invitation. In other kinds of case, also, the same is true. There is, for instance, the kind of criminal who commits offences as a way of denying unconscious feelings of inadequacy and inferiority engendered in him by early emotional neglect. Such feelings of inferiority have little in common with the more realistic sense of inadequacy which we all have when confronted by a difficult problem. For one thing, they are all-pervading: the individual feels, not merely unable to perform a particular task, but below-par as a person. Such feelings however are only vaguely, if at all, within his span of consciousness; he is aware only of a feeling of disquiet which makes him want to prove himself time after time. Criminals of this type commit offences in order to bolster up their own self-respect. Their crimes make them feel that they do count at last, and the longer their sentences (or the larger the headlines they achieve in the daily papers) the tougher and the more important they feel. But as in the case of the punishment-seeker, what they have hit upon is not a solution but a palliative. Their feelings of inferiority are unconscious, and continue unaffected by whatever they may achieve in the way of criminal notoriety.

. . . Some psycho-analysts are now raising the question of whether, especially in the case of crimes against the person like sexual assault and violence, the victim may not be as responsible for the offence as the person who perpetrates it. The crime, in other words, may be invited by the victim because it satisfies some unconscious wish in him. There is plenty of evidence of the existence of such symbiotic patterns. A familiar case is that of the wife who is constantly beaten by the husband, and who swears she will go away for good, but never does. Her friends cannot understand why she stays, but in spite of her frequent complaints, the ill-treatment she receives seems to satisfy her unconscious wish to be dominated and hurt, which itself dovetails fatally with her husband's need to have somebody to dominate and to hurt. The study of alcoholics shows that some are protected and even kept by their wives, who suffer a good deal in other ways, also, from their spouses' drunken behaviour. Yet they seem to need to have their husbands dependent upon them as much as their inadequate menfolk need them to lean upon. At the conscious level, such a woman may regret her marital lot, and indeed protest against it very loudly, but her real feelings show in the numerous obstacles she puts up against any treatment given to him, as well as the remarkable lack of emotion she shows in the face of one domestic fracas after another. Cases are not unknown in which any abatement of the husband's alcoholism as a result of treatment is followed by emotional disturbance or even breakdown on the part of the wife.

Is it likely then, that a person who is assaulted or raped may have unconsciously wanted this to happen? Clinical evidence suggests that this is sometimes so: the criminal has been seduced, as it were, into committing his crime. Even a little girl, sexually precocious, may occasionally have invited in some subtle way the sexual interference which aroused so much hostility in the rest of us towards her violators. Where this happens, to treat the criminal as solely responsible is as unjust as our present policy of punishing the prostitute but allowing her client to escape scot-free.

. . . In being punishers, our judges faithfully reflect the attitude of the general public. Criminals are butts on to whom the rest of us can discharge our own angry feelings. We all have such feelings, engendered by the frustrations of infancy, and the irritations of adult life may add to them. To discharge them upon our friends and neighbours is not permissible, at least unless they give us due cause. The criminal, on the other hand, is a sitting target. He has given us plenty of excuse. We can hate him and punish him with a positive sense of virtue.

The position is even more complicated than this. We all have unconscious wishes to keep under control, and at times of stress or temptation this is by no means easy. The common solution then is to see these wishes as if they were in other people and not in ourselves. In punishing them, we therefore reassure ourselves about our own innocence, and at the same time coerce ourselves into good behaviour. The conscious ego must often be saying, at a level of experience below the threshold of consciousness, 'See what will happen to you if you do that'. We are able to give a concrete demonstration of the dangers lying in wait for ourselves, unless we are good, and maintain our repressions intact.

From *Crime in a Changing Society* by Howard Jones

"Belting them across the ear is hardly calculated to solve their little problems, Miss Triceps."

4 Sex and young people

When boys and girls reach adolescence, most of them have had experiences of one sort or another relating to sex. These experiences include discovery of the anatomical differences between the sexes, an interest in childish forms of sex play, and curiosity about sex and reproduction.

. . . In a study by Ramsey (1943) it was found that 73 per cent of boys had had experience with masturbation by the age of twelve years, and 98 per cent had had such experience by the age of fifteen. By six years or even earlier, 5 per cent had had such experience, and at the age of nine, about 23 per cent. In Ramsey's population of boys, over half had experienced nocturnal emissions, or 'wet dreams', by the age of fifteen. Nocturnal emissions that occur during sleep come about without any deliberate action by the dreamer. A large percentage of boys had had ejaculations brought about by themselves or through sex play with others before they experienced wet dreams. By the age of thirteen, 38 per cent of the boys had been involved in homosexual play. Pre-adolescent sex play with girls or women appeared in two thirds of the histories, and one third of the boys had attempted heterosexual intercourse before adolescence.

Ramsey cites evidence from other studies tending generally to confirm his findings. While the exact percentages and proportions in this study and in others are not important, the significant finding is that a large number of boys are active sexually in one way or another prior to adolescence.

. . . Nearly all adolescent boys masturbate more or less frequently. During recent decades there has been a marked change in what is said and written about masturbation. The horrid and brutal threats of insanity, depravity, sterility, and hell fire once repeated in books on 'What Every Boy Should Know' have largely been removed. But there probably still is (or, at least, until recently there still was) a great deal of guilt and fear associated with masturbation. In a study of college men published in 1937, Pullias found that a majority of these had been told that serious physical and mental damage would result from masturbation, and a majority of them believed that some type of serious damage would ensue. As an extreme case, he speaks of a boy who said he could not become a lawyer as he had planned because his mind and personality had deteriorated as a result of masturbation. Pullias points out that the opinions of these college men were quite out of line with medical and psychological views concerning the harmfulness of the practice.

. . . It is early on in the teens, if not before, that the enterprising adolescent would like to begin to have dates or 'keep company'. Frequently young people, particularly the girls, would like to start 'going out' with members of the opposite sex before their parents are ready to give them permission to do so. In a study by G. F. Smith (1924), girls, in reporting the age at which they were first interested in 'going out' with boys, gave the range from ten to eighteen years. The median age was fourteen years. However, it was not until the median age of sixteen years that a girl got permission from her parents to keep company . . . W. M. Smith (1952) noted that there have been some changes in dating procedures during the past fifteen years. According to his findings, three fourths of city girls had had their first date before the age of fifteen; and 70 per cent of city boys and about 60 per cent of farm boys had had their first dates at sixteen or earlier.

As is true in connection with any new venture, the experiences adolescents have with dating are not without some difficulties. A study by Christensen (1952) of a large sampling of high school students showed that feelings ·of shyness in connection with dating were common among both boys and girls.

While we may assume that when a boy dates a girl or a girl a boy, they usually have a desire to go out together, motives other than a strong liking for each other also came into the picture. A study by Crist (1953) indicates that many adolescents enter into the early stages of dating partly because the group expects it and not solely because of personal interest.

. . . Mead (1949) has pointed out that while in our culture we have given up chaperoning young people and permit and even encourage them to get into situations where they can indulge in sex behavior, we have not relaxed our disapproval of the girl who becomes pregnant nor simplified the problems of the unmarried mother. She states that we, so to speak, give young people a setting for behavior for which we then punish them when it occurs. She notes particularly the differences that sometimes prevail in the attitudes of girls and boys. The boy is expected to ask as much as possible and the girl to yield as little as possible, and this often goes on for many years. The girl is supposed to provide a conscience for two, so to speak, until she is married, playing the game deftly, but playing it safe. Then, when married, she is supposed to make a complete about-face. The lot of the girl confronted with this dilemma is not an easy one.

. . . Attitudes an adolescent has toward himself and others are likely to be reflected in his sex conduct, even though many of these attitudes were not originally linked to his sexual development.

Some of the child's earliest experiences of being rejected are connected with his sexual development. If a child's elders are anxious about sex, regard it as dirty, are mortified when, for example, he plays with his genital organ, the child is being taught, so to speak, to regard a part of himself as something dirty and is taught to look upon his sex organs and his interest in manipulating them as something to be anxious about. If a child is taught not to have respect for a part of his body he is, in effect, being taught not fully to respect himself. If he is taught to view his sexual nature with shame he is taught to view a part of himself as shameful.

Sex comes into the flow of development in many other ways. If sex is looked upon as something strictly forbidden, it may become a weapon that the child (or older person) uses to disobey others and to show rebellion and defiance. One of the most emphatic means adolescent boys and girls can use to flaunt their parents is to become involved in sexual escapades their parents dread and have strictly forbidden. Sexual behavior may also become associated with punishment and aggressiveness and, when this occurs, a person may use sexual advances as a means of punishing or degrading or otherwise hurting someone else or himself.

Sex may also become entangled with other attitudes the adolescent has about himself and others. If he is unsure of himself, doubtful as to his manliness or adequacy, one way of trying to prove himself is to make sexual conquests. The boy and girl who have doubts about whether they are likable and acceptable persons may seek through one sexual exploit after another to remove these doubts. If they are insecure persons who need to prove their superiority over others they may show an intense competitiveness in their sexual behavior.

From *The Psychology of Adolescence* by Dr. Arthur T. Jersild

"Because since he read that he's been sitting here asking me a lot of fool questions—that's why."

London Express Service

Would you believe it?

It is always difficult to arrive at the truth about people's sexual behaviour. They do not always answer questions truthfully and even the experts can go wrong, as the following story shows:

Last week, a rare happening took place in the hot-house world of the sex-and-morals pundits. It revealed something of the mechanism of how doubtful or unsupported tales become elevated by quotation at professional conferences or solemn report in newspapers, into the unquestioned 'sociological' facts on which attitudes to morals are based. This time the Press found out.

It happened at the Easter conference of the Education Welfare Officers' National Association, in Sheffield. A member of the Association's executive, Mr. Albert Millington, told the conference of a disturbing happening in Manchester.

The detail was meticulous: a 13-year-old girl played truant from school and was found in bed at home with a man. The girl reassured her mother, 'I won't have a baby, mum, because I've been taking the pills you take.' The girl had been stealing mother's birth pills and substituting aspirins. Result: the girl did not become pregnant, but mother did.

The national dailies happily ran the story at face value, though there must have been some sneaking doubts about how birth pills, with their distinctive labelling and wrapping, could be mistaken for aspirins.

Then the following day, the *Sun* brought its doubts into the open—and exposed the story as just a hoary joke that had been bandied about for some time. Millington lamely confessed, 'I was told the story by another welfare officer and accepted it in good faith.'

On Friday, *Spectator* columnist Alan Brien recalled an earlier phase in the story's history. On February 12 this year he had published a round-up of contemporary folk myths sent to him by readers: the pill story was included, 'sent in' from all corners of the world.

E

Mr. Brien, however, appeared to believe that his was the first printed record of the story. In fact last October it had appeared in the zany London *Evening News* column written by the Earl of Arran.

Under the optimistic headline 'True Story' he had told the tale as having happened to a friend of a friend. But this time the mother returned unexpectedly from a *holiday*, and the teenager had not yet acquired the specific age of 13.

Where had Lord Arran got his information? 'The commissionaire at Northcliffe House," he confessed to Insight.

From an Insight feature in *The Sunday Times*

The facts?

Few properly conducted investigations have been made into the sexual behaviour of British teenagers. A notable exception was that carried out by the Central Council for Health Education. During the preparation of their report (which was published in 1965) they interviewed 1,873 young people between the ages of 15 and 19 over a period of three years. The principles of strict random sampling were used throughout: a list was obtained of every adolescent living in seven areas in Great Britain and every 20th name was selected for interview.

All the adolescents were seen alone in conditions which encouraged them to talk freely and in complete confidence. We considered the question of confidence so important that no case histories appear in the report and only the briefest quotations are used—nobody can possibly be identified.

As a result of experience during a pilot research and after intensive training, we found it was possible to reach the point where the interviewers could be reasonably sure they were getting truthful answers. One of the most pleasing advantages of studying this particular age group is that young people of today are more frank than is the case with older people.

. . . More than one in five (21 per cent) of the teenage boys and over one in ten (11 per cent) of the girls (aged fifteen to nineteen) that we interviewed had experienced sexual intercourse.

. . . Before the age of fourteen it is quite rare. Less than one in a hundred boys (0·9 per cent) and one in a thousand girls (0·1 per cent) have had experience of sexual intercourse. At fourteen the figures are not much higher: about one in fifty boys (2·3 per cent) and less than one in 200 girls (0·4 per cent) have had premarital intercourse. Although reports about unmarried mothers of thirteen and fourteen are distressing, it should be noted that such cases are very exceptional.

At the age of fifteen and sixteen the figures are still less than one in ten for both boys and girls. This suggests that the fears often expressed about the extensive sexual activities between schoolboys and schoolgirls may be exaggerated. Although every secondary school probably contains a few boys and girls who are sexually experienced, it is unlikely that they are more than a very small minority.

It is at seventeen that there is a sudden increase in the percentage for boys, but not for girls. At this age a quarter of all boys have experience of sexual intercourse, but this applies to less than an eighth of the girls. At nineteen one in three of the boys and nearly a quarter of the girls are sexually experienced. So premarital intercourse among teenagers is not uncommon, but it is not universal or even an activity in which the majority take part.

. . . Nearly all the girls (81 per cent) maintained that the boy on this first occasion was a 'steady'; 16 per cent described the first partner as an acquaintance and only 3 per cent said the boy was a pick-up, i.e., someone they had met on the same day that intercourse took place. The figures for the boys are more equally spread over these three categories, probably because their idea of a 'steady' is quite different from the definition the girls would give. In fact 45 per cent of the boys described their first partner as a steady, 34 per cent as an acquaintance, and 16 per cent as a pick-up; very few boys had their first experience with a prostitute. Although the girls may have been over-defensive when answering this question, even allowing for this, it seems likely that the first experience of intercourse for boys as well as girls was usually with a friend, and often with someone they knew very well.

. . . We were surprised to find that the first sexual intercourse was nearly always unpremeditated. The replies of the teenagers showed that very few of them had set out with the intention of having intercourse on that particular evening.

. . . This point was pursued still further when the sexually experienced teenagers were asked: 'Have you any idea why it happened?' This would be a difficult question for anyone to answer and naturally many of the replies were vague and inarticulate. But it was a good question because it forced the teenager to look back on this first episode, and the answers can be classified fairly easily into four main categories:

Reason given	Boys %	Girls %
Sexual appetite	46	16
In love	10	42
Curiosity	25	13
Drunk	3	9
Others	4	8
Don't know	12	12
Total	100	100

The replies reveal the big difference in attitude between the two sexes. The boys were more likely to reply that they were impelled by sexual desire, whereas the girls were more likely to say they were in love.

. . . A large number of boys and quite a few girls were driven towards their first experience for reasons that can best be summed up by the word *curiosity*. Admonitory articles in the Press and hand-wringing by well-known people have given some adolescents the impression that most teenagers are sexually experienced, and some of the boys and girls must have wondered why they were exceptional and if they were missing something.

. . . We asked all of the boys, inexperienced as well as

experienced, if they had a steady girl friend. Over a third of the boys said they had, and still more girls (58 per cent) said they had a steady boy friend.

The girls were much more likely to be engaged; 16 per cent of the girls compared with 4 per cent of the boys said they were engaged. This suggests there is a misunderstanding between many courting couples; the girl feels sure they are going to get married, but the boy thinks that he has not yet committed himself.

Among the girls who said they had steady boy friends, 15 per cent were having sexual intercourse with them; among the girls who were engaged, 37 per cent were having sexual intercourse with their fiancés. Among the boys who had steady girl friends, 41 per cent were having sexual intercourse with them; among the few boys who were engaged, 39 per cent were having sexual intercourse with their fiancées.

This suggests that a large number of the sexually experienced teenagers have premarital intercourse with very close friends, and often with the person they will eventually marry. This is confirmed by the fact that a third of the experienced boys and three-quarters of the experienced girls had sexual intercourse with one partner only during the year.

In addition to the engaged couples who decide to have sexual intercourse before their wedding day, there are also courting couples who decide to get married when the girl discovers that she is pregnant. This further increases the number of experienced teenagers who have premarital intercourse only with the person they will marry. It seems likely that much of the premarital sexual activity of teenagers is not promiscuous behaviour.

From an article by Michael Schofield in *The Sunday Times*

Just two bodies rubbing madly . . .

Below is a further quotation from the conversation between a BBC talks producer and a young man of nineteen,
the first part of which was given on page 29. The producer
is now asking him about the group of beatniks to which he
at one time belonged:

You were with a fairly definite little group of people?
In a sense it wasn't a little group; it's a tremendous sort
of password, you know, being a beatnik. You go into any
town; I used to go to Cornwall quite a lot and walk into
St. Ives, and you'd see people dressed slightly like you,
with the same attitude, and you'd think 'Oh, well, there's
everybody else, what do I care about the world?'
What about sex? Was there much sex in this world?
Quite a lot, yes. I suppose the idea was if there was any
virginity around it was your chance to stuff it. The first
real sex experience I had was when I was eleven with a girl
exactly the same age. But that was sort of exploration, I
didn't really know what was going on. And when I was
fifteen, I went out with a girl who had lost her virginity
when she was thirteen. She was the same age as me. I
went out with her for about six months, and I first started
sleeping with her. And from that time onwards any girl
that I was going out with I usually ended up by jumping
into bed with her.
Did this give you much satisfaction?
Well, it depends what you mean by satisfaction. It was
just the normal behaviour: if you go out with a girl then
you end up by sleeping with her. And if I didn't, it didn't
bother me too much; and if I did, well, then I did, you
know.
*But would you regard yourself as being sexually precocious
in any way, would you say you were exceptional or was this
normal?*
It depends which standards you're measuring by. With
the group I was around with, it was the norm. Everybody
accepted this sort of behaviour. You're quite sensible about

it sometimes, you actually took precautions if you felt like it. But I suppose, by normal standards, it was precocious.

Did sex ever become boring?

In a sense, it did. I suppose I've become quite cynical about it now. I think there's nothing there but just two bodies rubbing madly in the dark, you know, and there's no relationship between them, no consideration; but I don't think it has ever become boring, although I've had, I suppose, a fair amount of experience.

Are there any girls that you felt strongly for, apart from the bodies rubbing together? I mean, was there anyone you felt fond of?

Oh, yes, quite a few, in lots of different ways. Three girls, I suppose, in my life, in the past four years, I've felt quite strongly for; one I went out with for two years, went round on holiday together, went to Cornwall together; we were around the scene together, then we broke up. I went out with another one who waited for me when I was in the detention centre. I've never been able to find out what my feelings are about a girl. I don't know, I get the idea, as soon as you say 'I love you' it doesn't mean anything any more, because you're thinking about it; it's not natural behaviour. As soon as you start talking about the ideas of romantic love, and being in love with somebody all the time and having to be in love with them all the time, all feeling goes. If you don't talk about it, then I think you get on quite well.

But you wouldn't apply this to most of the group that you were with at that time? With most of them, it was just sex and nothing else?

No, I don't think it was, because although sex was pretty common and everybody would sleep with everybody else, there was generally quite a lot of feeling involved, even if it was only temporary: people would make quite strong relationships, even when they were fifteen or sixteen.

Marriage was regarded as a kind of death, was it? I mean, there was no such thing as marriage?

No, not at all. Lots of my friends, who were the same age as me, they're married now. It's true a lot of them have broken up, but marriage certainly wasn't death, it was accepted. This was something that you did.

Were you still accepted in the group?

Oh, yes. Quite a few people got married simply because they made their girl-friends pregnant and they decided well, they may as well. Most of them have broken up, as I say.

From *The Listener*

What's all the fuss about?

An interview with Jack O'Donovan, 20, of Seaforth, Liverpool 21:

'What's all the fuss about? Boys have been going out with girls ever since Adam. And the chasers have always been the girls, always, from Eve onwards. Well, what has happened? This has now come into the open. Girls start off by openly worshipping any boy with a guitar and a wiggle capable of getting up on a stage and releasing her urges. Right, it doesn't end there. Not every girl can get herself a Beatle—there aren't even enough tenth-rate pop artists available. So they get themselves all worked up at places like the Cavern and then turn like hungry tigresses on the nearest available fellow. It stands to reason doesn't it? So now the lads just sit back and wait for the rush. We don't even have to pretend to chase them any more.

'Now the next question is how to cope with the manna that's dropping out of the sky. It's unfair to expose fellows to all that temptation on the one hand and tell them they're not to handle the merchandise on the other. Teachers at school, parsons in their pulpits, are all blathering away about how wrong it is for young people to have any sexual intercourse before they're married. Nobody really holds with that sort of eye-wash any more, least of all the teachers and the parsons. It's just a lot of twaddle they talk in the hope of keeping the rates—and the birthrate—down. Ideally, according to them, young people should be seen and not heard. The moment they do something to draw attention to themselves, voom: trouble. They draw the wrath of God down on their heads—or the probation officer.

'Why don't they face up to the realities the way they're always telling us to do? For example, they should issue contraceptives free on the National Health. They should have clinics where young people can go for medical advice *before* it's too late. I've not had it myself, but blokes I know who've had venereal disease say the medical orderlies at the clinics are instructed to make things as unpleasant as possible for the patients—to put them off from getting another dose. It often serves only to put them off from going there again and trying to treat themselves or go to some back-alley quack and not being properly checked out.

'Instead of all this furtive stuff, boys and girls should be encouraged to drop into those clinics without any more fuss attached to it than going into a chemist's shop for a headache powder. The people running the clinics should be trained to be nice and open-minded towards their patients. A smile never did nobody any harm, and there's too much Victorian prissiness still in the medical profession. They're class-ridden to high hell. A professional man's daughter can be put up for pod and buy herself a discreet abortion, while a working-class girl has to take the rap as an unmarried mother and be made an outcast. There's too much hypocrisy going around in the medical profession. Let them have an open policy towards the sex problems of the young.

'Nobody is going to prevent sexual intercourse from going on between young men and women, here or anywhere else. So why not move with the times, eh?'

From *Generation X* by Charles Hamblett and Jane Deverson

5 Getting married

There have been many studies of the characteristics boys and girls seek in a person whom they are dating or might think of marrying. Mather (1934) in an investigation of the 'courtship ideals' of high school youth, found that among the characteristics named most often by both boys and girls were 'real brains' and good looks. 'Good looks' were given a higher rating by boys as desirable in a girl than by girls as something desirable in a boy. In some ways it appears that girls are more mature when they specify what they want in a boy. Girls, for example, gave a greater emphasis to considerateness than did boys. In a study by Christensen (1947) both boys and girls emphasised such character traits as dependability and emotional maturity in naming the characteristics of a desirable mate. The boys gave relatively greater emphasis to youthfulness, attractiveness, and popularity. Girls, on the other hand, gave greater emphasis to such traits as financial ability, education, ambition, and similarity of backgrounds.

. . . Maslow (1953) states that in observing several 'relatively healthy' young college men and women he has noted that the more mature they become, the less attracted they are by such characteristics as 'handsome,' 'good-looking,' 'good dancer,' 'nice breasts,' 'physically strong,' 'tall,' 'good necker,' and the more they speak of compatibility, goodness, decency, good companionship, considerateness. He notes a tendency with greater maturity to speak of a person to whom one is attracted in terms of the character of this person rather than in terms of physical traits.

. . . In the usual course of events it seems rarely to happen that two adolescents meet and then love each other (and no one else before or after) with equal intensity and go on to live happily ever after. Matters do not usually progress with such comfort, equality, speed, and finality.

Judging from available findings, the average young person falls in love not once but several times during early and late adolescent years.

. . . We cannot say it is a good thing or not a good thing for a given adolescent to fall in love just once, or a few times, or many times. We can say, however, that the impulses and feelings that underlie the typical young person's need to love are so strong that he or she will be enterprising in seeking someone to love and will probably be able to go on to share love with someone else even if this or that venture into love does not succeed or does not last. Actually, it is probably far less important for an adolescent to fall in love several times and to have the opportunity to make comparisons between several partners than to possess the degree of self-knowledge and emotional maturity that makes it possible for him to be aware of what he is seeking and to appreciate the value of a healthy love relationship, if he has been fortunate enough to find it.

. . . Among the components of being in love are feelings of tenderness, an impulse to cherish, comfort, and protect, a desire to do things that will bring joy to the other person. In these sentiments there is a large amount of other-centeredness. They are what distinguishes what is known as 'true love' from an infatuation consisting primarily of physical appetite or a desire simply to possess someone else. These sentiments give the state of being in love an aspect of unselfishness. The gratification that comes through the exercise of tenderness comes through the medium of having taken thought of someone else. It involves a disposition to *give* emotionally, rather than simply to take.

. . . However, the persons who are in love may be so overwhelmed by their feelings that they become blind to faults or conditions that in time would create unhappiness. The person who is in love may overlook bad habits, weaknesses of character, symptoms of emotional immaturity, that to a disinterested onlooker do not bode well for the future. Similarly overlooked may be differences in background, ideals, age, station in life, religious affiliation, and other social and cultural conditions which, in time, may require very difficult and perhaps insurmountable practical and psychological adjustments.

The average age at which men and women marry for the first time has declined during recent years (Bossard,

1956). Many adolescents marry soon after high school or even while they are still in high school, and many others marry while in college or while yet of college age. The average age of first marriage is about twenty years for women and twenty-two years for men.

When adolescents marry they are expected to accept each other for better or for worse. They probably hope, if all goes well, to live happily ever afterward. Many marriages are permanent, and many report they are happy in their marriages. But some are not happy. Many who hoped to find happiness later conclude they would be happier if the marriage were undone.

In recent years, according to estimates published by the Bureau of the Census (1955) the number of divorces in the United States has been about a fourth of the total number of marriages. The divorce rate varies considerably in different sections of the country. Apart from divorces, there are many incompatible persons who are separated (see, e.g., Davis, 1952 and Bossard, 1956). And among those who are living together, there are many who do not regard their marriages as being particularly happy. As might be expected, marriage, like any other human institution, has its tensions, and the married relationship, like any human relationship, has its stresses and strains.

. . . The conditions that impel young people to marry at an early age do not necessarily give them the kind of emotional and social maturity and the kind of practical competence that the responsibilities of married life demand. There may be many influences that lead a young person to seek marriage before he or she is prepared for it, including the pressure of customs in the community, a desire to escape from home, a hope of gaining through another person a kind of emotional security he or she has not been able to achieve alone, a desire to escape from loneliness, a need to prove his or her adequacy as a man or woman, a need to make what seems to be a good match by marrying someone who at the moment seems to be glamorous, and the like.

The trend toward earlier marriages, coupled with a high rate of broken marriages, underscores the fact that young people need as much help as they can get to prepare themselves for the venture into married life. Although there probably is no kind of preparation that would guarantee happy marriages, or eliminate broken marriages or incompatibility in marriage, it is reasonable to assume that underlying some of the marriages that turn out unhappily there have been social pressures, practical difficulties, and emotional problems that young people could be helped to understand and face more realistically than they commonly do. In preparing for marriage, or for any other aspect of adult life, anything that can be done to help the young person to understand himself and others, and to face the practical issues and the emotional currents that influence his attitudes towards himself and others would be likely, at least to some degree, to be of some value.

From *The Psychology of Adolescence* by Dr. Arthur T. Jersild

Young people's opinions

Michael Boulton, age 20, 45 Roundway, Blearton, Stoke-on-Trent:

'I go to dances at weekends with the lads, and I must admit I'm a bit of a flirt sometimes. I like to be with people. I don't know what to do with myself when I'm alone.

'I went steady for a year at one time, and I'd go steady again if I could find the right girl. I always find something wrong with the girl, or she finds something wrong with me. The last girl I had had to be in by 10.30 so I packed her in. I couldn't stand it, it was no good.

'I don't want a fancy girl, just a nice ordinary lass. Really nice-looking girls can have all the dates they want, they can go wild and flirt around because they know they're attractive. I don't want a girl like that, she'd be too much of a handful—not worth the trouble. No, all I want is a girl who will be faithful to me and enjoy my company—a really decent girl.

'I don't like girls in groups. When they go to dances in a crowd they dance by themselves and won't dance with   67 you. I think it's ridiculous, girls dancing with girls. I don't like sitting watching all the time and yet I feel terrible when a girl refuses to dance with me.

'When that happens I lose my nerve and become afraid to ask anyone else. So I have to go to the bar and have a few drinks. That brings my nerve back. But if a girl doesn't turn up for a date I have the attitude, well, there are plenty more fish in the sea.

'Marriage is the only thing which really scares me. With the right girl I suppose it's okay, but I couldn't imagine myself having a house and a wife. I like to feel free, to go anywhere and not have to worry. That's one nice thing about not having a girl friend, you're free to go out and enjoy yourself with the lads. Having a girl ties you down.

'The more you go out with a girl, the more involved you get. I'm frightened of becoming engaged. That would finish me—because I'd never break off an engagement, it isn't fair on the girl. Too many teenagers rush into marriage. They don't know what they're missing. I thought my first love was marvellous, then I discovered the girl was an incurable flirt and I packed her in.

'Next time I have a steady girl I'm going to make it clear from the start that I want a free night off with the lads every week. Once you lose all your friends, you're stuck to the girl and you've had it.

'Mind you, you can never trust a girl. When you have a night off with the lads, you don't know what she's doing. She could be out with another feller for all you know.

'But still, I'm happy. Twenty is a really good age. I enjoy myself now, and I'm much happier than I was in my teens— more sure of myself.'

Ralph Tate, age 25, 105 Alderton Heights, Leeds 17:

'Nearly all my friends are married, but I'm a bachelor type myself. I go out with quite a lot of girls, I take them out for drinks, to the cinema or dancing and I enjoy their company. But girls always want to get married and when that subject is brought up I don't want to see them any more. I feel bad about it when I look back, but the longer you go out with a girl, the more complicated it becomes. So I break it off as soon as a girl starts to get fond of me. It's kinder that way.

' Went out with a girl for two years and nearly got caught. I hate feeling tied down. You can't go out every night when you're married, and a couple soon start getting browned off with each other. The man starts going out with his mates, and then the trouble starts. Marriage isn't a thing to rush into. It's a very serious thing and you've got to think carefully about it. You've got to say to yourself "I'm married, and that's it. I can't go out with the boys any more."

'It's easy to meet girls. I don't chase them, but I wouldn't be normal if I didn't like them. I don't fall in love easily. In fact I only fell in love once and the girl was married, so there was nothing I could do. I keep thinking about her, and I compare all the girls I meet to her. They're never as good—and I suppose that's why I haven't fallen for anyone else.'

From *Generation X* by Charles Hamblett and Jane Deverson

The Marriage Service

according to the Book of Common Prayer (1662) of the Church of England

¶ *At the day and time appointed for solemnisation of Matrimony, the persons to be married shall come into the body of the church with their friends and neighbours: and there standing together, the man on the right hand, and the woman on the left, the Priest shall say,*

DEARLY beloved, we are gathered together here in the sight of God, and in the face of this congregation, to join together this man and this woman in Holy Matrimony; which is an honourable estate, instituted of God in the time of man's innocency, signifying unto us the mystical union that is betwixt Christ and his Church; which holy estate Christ adorned and beautified with his presence, and first

69

miracle that he wrought, in Cana of Galilee; and is commended of Saint Paul to be honourable among all men: and therefore is not by any to be enterprised, nor taken in hand, unadvisedly, lightly, or wantonly, to satisfy men's carnal lusts and appetites, like brute beasts that have no understanding; but reverently, discreetly, advisedly, soberly, and in the fear of God; duly considering the causes for which Matrimony was ordained.

First, It was ordained for the procreation of children, to be brought up in the fear and nurture of the Lord, and to the praise of his holy Name.

Secondly, It was ordained for a remedy against sin, and to avoid fornication; that such persons as have not the gift of continency might marry, and keep themselves undefiled members of Christ's body.

Thirdly, It was ordained for the mutual society, help, and comfort, that the one ought to have of the other, both in prosperity and adversity.

Into which holy estate these two persons present come now to be joined. Therefore if any man can shew any just cause, why they may not lawfully be joined together, let him now speak, or else hereafter for ever hold his peace.

And also, speaking unto the persons that shall be married, he shall say,

I REQUIRE and charge you both, as ye will answer at the dreadful day of judgement when the secrets of all hearts shall be disclosed, that if either of you know any impediment, why ye may not be lawfully joined together in Matrimony, ye do now confess it. For be ye well assured, that so many as are coupled together otherwise than God's Word doth allow are not joined together by God; neither is their Matrimony lawful.

At which day of Marriage, if any man do allege and declare any impediment, why they may not be coupled together in Matrimony, by God's law, or the laws of this Realm; and will be bound, and sufficient sureties with him, to the parties; or else put in a caution (to the full value of such charges as the persons to be married do thereby sustain) to prove his allegation; then the solemnisation must be deferred, until such time as the truth be tried.

If no impediment be alleged, then shall the Curate say unto the man,

N. WILT thou have this woman to thy wedded wife, to live together after God's ordinance in the holy estate of Matrimony? Wilt thou love her, comfort her, honour, and keep her, in sickness and in health; and forsaking all other, keep thee only unto her, so long as ye both shall live?

The man shall answer,
I will. ᴨₒᵗ

Then shall the Priest say unto the woman,

N. WILT thou have this man to thy wedded husband, to live together after God's ordinance in the holy estate of Matrimony? Wilt thou obey him, and serve him, love, honour, and keep him, in sickness and in health; and, forsaking all other, keep thee only unto him, so long as ye both shall live?

The woman shall answer,
I will. ᛁ ᶠᵘ

Then shall the Minister say,
Who giveth this woman to be married to this man?

Then shall they give their troth to each other in this manner.

The Minister receiving the woman at her father's or friend's hands, shall cause the man with his right hand to take the woman by her right hand, and to say after him as followeth.

I N. take thee N. to my wedded wife, to have and to hold from this day forward, for better for worse, for richer for poorer, in sickness and in health, to love and to cherish, till death us do part, according to God's holy ordinance; and thereto I plight thee my troth.

Then shall they loose their hands; and the woman, with her right hand taking the man by his right hand, shall likewise say after the Minister,

I N. take thee N. to my wedded husband, to have and to hold from this day forward, for better for worse, for richer for poorer, in sickness and in health, to love, cherish, and to obey, till death us do part, according to God's holy ordinance; and thereto I give thee my troth.

Then shall they again loose their hands; and the man shall give unto the woman a ring, laying the same upon the book with the accustomed duty to the Priest and Clerk. And the Priest, taking the ring, shall deliver it unto the man, to put it upon the fourth finger of the woman's left hand. And the man holding the ring there, and taught by the Priest, shall say,

W ITH this ring I thee wed, with my body I thee worship, and with all my worldly goods I thee endow; In the name of the Father, and of the Son, and of the Holy Ghost. Amen.

¶ *Then the man leaving the ring upon the fourth finger of the woman's left hand, they shall both kneel down; and the Minister shall say,*

Let us pray.

O ETERNAL God, Creator and Preserver of all mankind, giver of all spiritual grace, the author of everlasting life: Send thy blessing upon these thy servants, this man and this woman, whom we bless in thy name; that, as Isaac and Rebecca lived faithfully together, so these persons may surely perform and keep the vow and covenant betwixt them made, (whereof this ring given and received is a token and pledge,) and may ever remain in perfect love and peace together, and live according to thy laws; through Jesus Christ our Lord. *Amen.*

Then shall the Priest join their right hands together, and say,

Those whom God hath joined together let no man put asunder.

Then shall the Minister speak unto the people.

F ORASMUCH as N. and N. have consented together in holy wedlock, and have witnessed the same before God and this company, and thereto have given and pledged their troth either to other, and have declared the same by giving and receiving of a ring, and by joining of hands; I pronounce that they be man and wife together, In the name of the Father, and of the Son, and of the Holy Ghost. Amen.

Then follow the blessing, a psalm, prayers, and a reading or sermon.

An Alternative Form of the Marriage Service

taken from the Prayer Book of 1928

There are two significant changes in this version of the marriage service.

First, the second purpose of marriage is reworded. Instead of, 'It was ordained for a remedy against sin, and to avoid fornication; that such persons as have not the gift of continency might marry, and keep themselves undefiled members of Christ's body', it becomes, 'It was ordained in order that the natural instincts and affections, implanted by God, should be hallowed and directed aright; that those who are called of God to this holy estate should continue therein in pureness of living'.

Secondly, the woman's promise is changed. Instead of being asked, 'Wilt thou obey him, and serve him, love, honour, and keep him, in sickness and in health . . .', she is asked, 'Wilt thou love him, comfort him, honour and keep him, in sickness and in health . . .'

In addition, certain old-fashioned words (such as 'ordinance') are replaced by more modern ones (such as 'law') and expressions like 'men's carnal lusts and appetites' are omitted.

Should non-believers be married in church?

Here are two further extracts from interviews with young people:

'I've been to friends' weddings and I feel out of place in a church. I think religion is a farce.'

'Religion to most teenagers is an old person's fairytale. Most teenagers think about God but the Bible and the church seems so completely remote and irrelevant to their lives, that they cannot take them seriously. The Church has no meaning—a place full of old ladies in felt hats and smelling of cats and Pekinese. Boring sermons, meaningless prayers.

'Everything they see around them is completely irreligious. Being "expected" to believe in God is ridiculous. Religion is for old people who have given up living and so need this fantasy about a better life hereafter. It's not for young people who want to live, explore, find out about life for themselves.

'The rituals are so ludicrous. Television has opened our eyes to the pantomime and mumbo-jumbo of organised religious ceremony. What's the difference between a crowd of worshippers in St. Peter's Square getting a puerile wave of the hand from their "Papa" and a Borneo cannibal having a witchdoctor waving a human thighbone over his woolly head? Some people genuflect to plaster statues of the Virgin Mary while others talk to palm trees. Big deal.'

74   From *Generation X* by Charles Hamblett and Jane Deverson

6 Woman's place

The man, more robust, is fitted for severe labour, and for field exercise; the woman, more delicate, is fitted for sedentary occupations, and particularly for nursing children. The man, bold and vigorous, is qualified for being a protector; the woman, delicate, and timid, requires protection. Hence it is that a man never admires a woman for possessing bodily strength or personal courage; and women always despise men who are totally destitute of these qualities. The man, as a protector, is directed by nature to govern; the woman, conscious of inferiority, is disposed to obey. Their intellectual powers correspond to the destination of nature. Men have penetration and solid judgment to fit them for governing, women have sufficient understanding to make a decent figure under a good government; a greater portion would excite dangerous rivalry between the sexes, which nature has avoided by giving them different talents. Women have more imagination and sensibility than men which make all their enjoyments more exquisite; at the same time that they are better qualified to communicate enjoyment. Add another capital difference of disposition: The gentle and insinuating manners of the female sex tend to soften the roughness of the other sex; and wherever women are indulged with any freedom, they polish sooner than men.

These are not the only particulars that distinguish the sexes. With respect to the ultimate end of love, it is the privilege of the male, as superior and protector, to make a choice; the female preferred has no privilege but barely to consent or to refuse . . . Among all nations it is the practice for men to court, and for women to be courted; and were the most beautiful woman on earth to invert this practice, she would forfeit the esteem, however by her external grace she might excite the desire, of the man whom she addressed. The great moral virtues which may be comprehended under the general term integrity are all absolutely necessary to make either men or women estimable; but to procure esteem to the female character, the modesty peculiar to their sex is a very essential circumstance. Nature hath provided them with it as a defence against the artful solicitations of the other sex before marriage, and also as a support of conjugal fidelity.

From the fourth edition (1800-10) of the
Encyclopaedia Britannica

Women in China

Who decides that some jobs are to be done by men and others by women? Can old ideas be changed?

Of all the changes imposed in China by Peking's Communist regime over the past 15 years perhaps the most significant has been the alteration of Chinese women. Ideally, at least, the graceful, willowy figure of yore has become a severe, almost sexless silhouette leaning over a lathe or immersed knee-high in an irrigation ditch.

Undeniably, the Chinese female has been 'emancipated'. According to official Communist statistics, the number of women employed in industry has increased tenfold since 1950. More than 60 per cent of Shanghai's textile workers are women—and 173 of them are factory directors.

In heavy industries, such as the Anshan Steel Works, there are some 400 women engineers and technicians. About 500 women serve as factory managers and foremen in the machine-building industry.

Among the Chinese heroines is Chen Chih-ying, who once supported her family by collecting rubbish, and is now deputy chief of staff of a Chinese Air Force unit. Another is Chang Tsai-wei, an engineer at a Dairen railway plant, who helped design a 4,000-horsepower locomotive. Production team leader Chou Lien of Kwangtung province recently broke her country's record for transplanting rice sprouts.

. . . In the Communists' dynamic drive to turn Chinese women into Socialist pin-ups it is, of course, difficult to separate propaganda from fact. The evidence is abundant, however, that despite official pressures, ladies will be ladies.

As such, they seem to follow their natural instincts.

Judged from various accounts, many young urban females have lately shown a dangerous drift towards 'bourgeois' fashion in their dress and manner. They seem anxious in many cases to lay their hands on cosmetics. In Shanghai a policeman recently reported the horrifying appearance of girls in tight slacks and pointed shoes. One young lady, who blossomed out in an open-neck blouse, was summarily dismissed as being 'wrong in the head'.

Similarly, Chinese publications constantly discuss the dilemma of women torn between revolutionary love for Socialism and individualistic love for husband and family. Such publicity is clearly aimed at encouraging political dedication and yet, inadvertently, it reveals the tug of emotions pulling at Chinese women.

A girl called Ho Fang raised the problem not long ago in a letter to *Women of China,* a Chinese monthly magazine. Two years before, she recounted, she had fallen in love with Wang Jen, a Young Communist League member in her factory. She found him a 'good comrade'—but not 'my ideal lover'.

In fact, she found him 'monotonous, unfeeling, lacking in fun'. She complained that he spent his spare time reading about 'production techniques'. He chided her for wanting to see films, dance or dine in restaurants, urging that 'the energy of young people should be utilised in exhaustive work, in order to contribute something to Socialist construction'.

Inevitably she turned away to another youth, Hsiao Li— a 'very ardent, broadminded' chap, as Ho Fang described him. He wined and dined her, gave her woollens and a wrist-watch, took her strolling in the park and generally showed her a grand time.

But fun-loving Hsiao Li, acknowledged the girl, was an inadequate worker with low political consciousness. Thus her problem: should she marry tried and trusted Wang Jen and take the dull, straight and narrow road to revolution? Or should she slide merrily down the bourgeois primrose path with Hsiao Li?

Predictably, most readers advised Ho Fang to choose 77

Wang Jen. As one wrote: 'Get rid of old ideas, firmly put politics in the commanding position, and choose the revolutionary partner.'

And yet, in the entire lovelorn exercise—perhaps completely contrived by the Communist authorities—there is the recognition that the liberated woman is a problem. Just as the capitalist world discovered a generation or more ago.

From a report by Stanley Karnow for the
Observer Foreign News Service

The Big Switch

How would you like to live in a world ruled by women? This is the position in Muriel Box's novel 'The Big Switch' when Dr. David Thornhill wakes up on April 25th 2078 to find that he has been lying unconscious in a refrigerated coffin since 1975. Originally he had entered the coffin as an experiment, intending to be released within 48 hours, but during that time there was a hydrogen bomb attack and his coffin was buried in the debris.

In the new world he wakes up to, women have taken over the government and all the responsible jobs. Men, who no longer have the vote, are expected to stay at home and look after the house and children. In the extract below, David meets the woman barrister, Auriol Spain, at the house of Fabia Holland (who was the woman archaelogist who dug him up) and her husband Philip.

David saw her as soon as he was halfway down the stairs.

He had washed and brushed his hair and then hung around the bedroom for twenty minutes or so before he could summon up courage to launch himself again on these strange, uncharted waters.

When he did, there she was, stretched out on a chaise longue in the entrance hall below. He took in the general picture at one glance and then started to concentrate on the details. Beginning, naturally, at the diamanté glitter of her tiny shoes and working his way up. The legs were good—very good—and the stockings the sheerest he had ever seen.

The clothes were odd, but he supposed that was the fashion. She wore a crimson satin suit, rather masculine in cut, but with a three-quarter-length jacket which he could only describe as eighteenth century in style. This she wore over a flowered yellow silk waistcoat, which contrived to conceal, and at the same time reveal, all the curves that were necessary and desirable. But it was when his gaze moved up to the firm chin, the full red lips, the tip-tilted nose and the large brown eyes, which appeared to be smiling especially for him, that he decided he was face to face with the most beautiful girl he had ever seen. And he had seen plenty—even if it had been a hundred years ago.

A low, slightly husky voice said: 'Hallo, there! You must be Doctor Thornhill. Come and sit down, won't you? I'm Auriol Spain.'

David stammered out a slightly strangled 'How do you do?' and was then saved by the precipitate appearance of Philip from the kitchen.

'Ah! I thought I heard voices. Doctor Thornhill, this is Auriol Spain, my niece. She's a barrister and some people find her amusing. At the moment, I must admit I don't. She's invited herself to dinner without giving anybody notice and I don't mind telling you Adrian (*the cook*) is quite furious. If we get any sort of dinner at all we'll be lucky. While I'm coping with that, she'll have to entertain you.

'It'll be a pleasure,' said the vision on the sofa.

'Fabia will be back soon—she just had to drive into town for some meeting or other.' He turned to David. 'I'd better warn you—Auriol's not only the most eligible and confirmed bachelor in town—she's a bit of a wolf, too! So you'd better watch out!'

With which he bustled out again.

'Come and sit here,' said Auriol, patting the seat of a chair close beside her. 'Fabia should have told me more about you. You're not in the least what I expected. And I must say you look very young for your age! How do you like the twenty-first century?'

'I feel a fish out of water at the moment.'

'That's only to be expected, isn't it? After all it is a bit of a change from the Mad Age.'

'The *Mad Age?*'

'Haven't you heard it called that before? It's the name our history books give to the sixty-one years from 1914 to 1975.'

'Really. Why?'

'Surely that's obvious to anyone. Don't you agree that was the period when practically everyone behaved as though he was completely insane?'

'I hadn't noticed it.'

'Oh come! In 1914 you had a world war—ten million men killed or maimed. Then the Roaring Twenties, the Great Depression, strikes, riots, Nazis, war in Spain, war in Ethiopia, war in Albania—finally another world war! More depressions, more wars—in Korea, Algeria, Indo-China, Africa—oh, I can't be bothered to list them all. And then, to top it all, H-Day. And nobody did anything about it! Just put up with it! How sane does that sound to you?'

'Not very, when you put it like that.'

'Exactly. Hence the Mad Age . . . But look, I'm talking too much. Typical lawyer, you see?'

'I wouldn't call you typical.'

'No? Why not?'

'I suppose because you're quite unique in my experience.'

'How charming! Do go on!' she gave him an encouraging smile.

'Would you mind if I asked you a question?'

'Not in the least.'

'Why did Philip refer to you as a bachelor?'

'Because I am one.' She looked at him quizzically. 'Anything wrong with that?'

'No—except that in the Mad Age we'd have called you a spinster.'

Auriol's laugh was like a peal of muted bells, he decided.

'I do know the word, but of course it's obsolete now. Practically archaic. A lot of things have changed since 1970, you know.'

'I'm beginning to find that out. Could I ask you something else? What exactly was the Big Switch?'

Auriol looked at him incredulously. 'You don't know?'

'Nobody seems to want to tell me.'

Auriol touched his hand lightly with hers. 'You poor lamb,' she said. 'Now me, I'd love to tell you all about it— and anything else you'd like to know!'

Auriol explains that the Big Switch had taken place in 1980. Many more women than men had been able to take shelter and so had survived the H-Bomb attacks. Because of this, a civil servant, Jean Ironside, had been able to seize control, using only women as her assistants. She had blamed all the troubles of the past on to men. Auriol continues:

'. . . So the only hope of building a world of peace and security was to see that men had no say in the government of it. The manmade world must go and in its place there must be a new world, run by women, controlled by women, in which the previous order of the sexes must be completely reversed—' Auriol paused dramatically—'In fact,' she ended, 'the Big Switch!'

There was silence for a moment as David began to take this in. Then he turned to her.

'And that's what happened?'

'Of course. Oh, it wasn't as simple and easy as it sounds. There was opposition from the men—naturally. There was even opposition from break-away groups of women. The men tried to use force. But the women were ready for that, because Jean Ironside had warned them to expect it. Still there were riots and bloodshed before it was through, but in the end women had their way. They were bound to— because Jean Ironside had spent months and years organising it. She was ready; the men weren't. She had the staff and the communications and the power; the men had already lost it. Women everywhere took a solemn vow not to allow the reins of government to get into the hands of men ever again. Henceforth it was going to be a woman's world, run by women. And that, my dear boy, is exactly what it is.'

David could not trust himself to say anything for a moment. He noticed that she was smiling at him sympathetically.

'Don't look so woebegone! It's not as bad as it sounds. Men can still have a good time—a very good time!—but they can't hold any position which might give them undesirable power. They've become the gentle sex, the leisured sex. The workers of the world are women. The Big Switch is fact.'

David was still silent and she looked at him a little anxiously. 'I hope it hasn't been too much of a shock?'

'No,' he said slowly. 'It explains a great deal . . . And I suppose I'll get used to it in time. There's only one thing I don't quite understand—'

'Tell me!'

'I can't see why the male sex should be blamed for everything that went wrong. Surely they did some good things, too? And surely, long before 1975, women could have voted themselves into office and taken at least a half share in the government if they'd really wanted to?'

'Granted. But you forget one thing. Women had been subjected to the male sex since the beginning of recorded history—with a few minor exceptions. They'd been conditioned to subservience for ages. It took a cataclysm to shake them out of that position. And it would take another to shake them back into it, now. Perhaps it's unjust that women should hold *all* the reins, but it was just as unfair when men held them—and remember they held them for literally thousands of years. It's really our turn now. So, like it or not, you've woken up to a woman's world. But it can be great fun for a man and it could be for you—if you'll let me have the pleasure of introducing you to it.'

He felt her hand suddenly resting on his with a pressure that was unmistakable—but before he could answer, the door was flung open and an angry-looking young man entered.

'Auriol!' he said. 'I didn't know you were here.'

Auriol withdrew her hand from David's and stood up. 'Jimmy! What brings you home?'

'If you really want to know, I've had the devil of a row with Claudia, and she's left me—and taken the children with her. Where's father? I've got to talk to him!'

Dinner in the Holland home that night was one of the

strangest meals David had ever sat through.

Auriol, in the chair next to his, contrived to keep him aware of her presence by touching his knee with hers from time to time and occasionally letting her hand rest lightly on his thigh for a moment or two. David had got the message by now—and didn't trouble to answer it.

The food which Adrian—who turned out to be a rather mousy little man in the early fifties, with a permanently petulant expression—served up to them was excellent. They washed it down with a wine that tasted exactly like a good claret, but which Fabia assured him was non-alcoholic. After that, David felt that it didn't taste quite so attractive after all, but he still drank his share.

It was the conversation, however, which made the meal memorable.

Jimmy was the centre of it from the beginning. There had been no time before dinner for Auriol to do more than introduce him as James Fanshaw, Philip's son. Now David, seated opposite him, noted that he was in the middle twenties, handsome and far less extravagantly dressed than his father. He talked rapidly, excitedly and extremely well. Altogether, not at all the sort of young man he would have expected to run home to mother—or rather, to father. And as he began to get the hang of the conversation, he realised that of course he was not.

Philip was the one most distressed about the matrimonial wrangle which had ended with Claudia picking up the two children from their school and leaving home with them.

'Haven't you any idea where she's taken them?' he asked his son anxiously.

'Oh, yes. They're at her parents' place.'

'How do you know?'

'I rang up, of course.'

'And what did Claudia say?'

'Only that she had no intention of coming back to me—nor of letting the children do so.'

'You haven't been having an affair with somebody else, have you?'

'Of course not. If you really want to know—'

But at this point Philip glanced at David and quickly   83

interrupted his son.

'I think we'd better talk about it privately later on,' he said. 'I'm sure Doctor Thornhill doesn't want to be regaled with your matrimonial disagreements.'

'Please don't stop on my account,' David told him. 'I'm on your stepson's side after all.'

As he said this, he felt Jimmy's eyes on him.

'What makes you think I'm Philip's stepson?' he asked.

'Your name, I suppose. If he were your father you'd bear his name, wouldn't you?'

'So I did, until I married. Fanshaw's my wife's name— damn her eyes!'

'You mean you took your wife's name when you married her?'

'Of course. Why not? Everyone does.'

David felt Auriol place her hand over his again as she broke in: 'You must remember, Jimmy, Doctor Thornhill hasn't caught up with all of our customs yet. In the Mad Age brides took their husbands' names.' She smiled up at David. 'The Big Switch changed all that.'

'I find it very hard to take.'

She looked at him mischievously. 'I don't see why you should. The woman, being the childbearer, is genetically speaking more important than the man. Why shouldn't she hand on her own name to her own posterity?'

Her hand was still resting on his and, looking down, David noticed that she wore no rings. Glancing round the table he observed that Fabia had none either, but that both Philip and Jimmy wore two rings apiece on the third fingers of their left hands.

'Tell me something else, while we're on the subject,' he said. 'Don't women wear wedding rings any more?'

'Good heavens, no! Engagement rings and wedding rings —they're for men! How else is a girl to tell whether a man's available or not?'

Jimmy looked shrewdly across the table and added: 'That's only just the beginning of it, you'll find. You'd better get used to the fact that women have various other little advantages, too. For instance, only they can own property. There's been a married man's property Bill before

Parliament three times, but they've always thrown it out. Oh yes—and the eldest daughter inherits the estate, not the eldest son as it used to be in your young days.'

'Oh dear,' sighed Philip. 'I do hope this isn't going to be one of those tiresome political evenings. Why can't we talk about something interesting for a change?'

'It is interesting to me, I can assure you,' David told him.

'Of course—I quite understand that. But I hope you won't let Jimmy unsettle you with all this talk. A man should be prepared to settle down to married life and concentrate on bringing up his children properly. What higher function in life could anyone ask?'

'The right to express himself?' Jimmy suggested. 'The right to work at what he's best fitted for?'

'Nobody's saying men shouldn't express themselves,' said his father, mildly. 'But they can do that without leaving the home and competing with women. A husband can take up music or poetry or writing—any of the arts in fact. If he wants physical exercise, there's nothing to stop him gardening, or playing tennis, or golf. But his chief duty is to make the home a place of peace and contentment for his wife and his children . . . And it's all very well for you to shake your head, Jimmy, but more freedom wouldn't be a good thing at all. As things are, men may appear to have the subordinate rôle, but you and I know perfectly well they're often the power behind the throne. Most women admit that they owe their success in life at least in part to their husbands—and only the other day Mrs. Hemingway, the boss of General Manufacturers, was telling me that when she takes on a new executive, she insists on interviewing the husband, too. A woman's value to her organisation is affected by the sort of husband she has— and a woman with an unreliable or unattractive husband just doesn't get the job.' He turned to David. 'I tell you, Doctor Thornhill, what we have to remember is that men are the artists and the poets of the world—always have been, always will be. Women are the realists—the materialistic sex. So let them get on with the job of managing the world and leave the men at home with their dreams.'

Jimmy had been muttering and shifting uncomfortably

85

in his chair during this, and now he burst out angrily. 'Damn their dreams! Can't you see what's happening right under your nose? We're being reduced to the level of a slave sex. Once we've done our job and impregnated our wives as often as they think necessary, we can spend the rest of our lives slaving away in the house. And when you talk about the arts, you just make me sick. You know perfectly well that Carstairs and Thompson and Stewart are all writing under female pseudonyms because that's the only way they can sell their books. I tell you, women won't even read a book if they think it's written by a man.'

Auriol's cool voice cut across Jimmy's anger. 'If that's the way you've been talking at home, Master Jimmy—especially in front of the children—I'm not surprised that Claudia walked out on you. And if you want me to take your case when it comes to court, you'll have to promise me not to start anything like that in front of the magistrate. Otherwise you haven't got a chance in hell of ever seeing your children again.'

From *The Big Switch* by Muriel Box

Andy Capp

7 Moving up in the world

'The Man Who Won the Pools' is a novel about a young electrician, Phil Tombs, who wins almost a quarter of a million on the pools. The story sheds some light on the workings of our class system. Here is how it starts:

'Twenty Camels, please,' Phil Tombs said, and put down two half crowns. He put them down as if he was saying here was the end of his old life. And the fags would certainly take most of the second two-and-six. He was still dazed—still after all this checking and telegram-sending and waiting —and his mind was working queerly. Twenty camels. Fifty elephants. A hundred houris. Anything money can buy. It was a comedy—or it would be a comedy if he wasn't frightened of it.

'Camels, did you say?' The girl behind the counter accompanied the sauce of her arched eyebrows with a sharp glance. She was thinking there was nothing out of the way in a chap like him buying Yank cigarettes. She was thinking his kind often had more money than the Varsity lot. Only she was thinking he had made this particular demand so offhandedly he must be doing something rash.

Tombs seeing this in the young woman's mind felt panic again as he thought how wrong she was. He said, short but civil:

'Yes, please.'

She slapped down the fags and slapped down his change. It was a sixpence.

'Quite going it, aren't we?' she asked sarcastically.

He saw she was surprising herself, making a pass like this. It was a class tobacconist's, next door to one of the big colleges. Sometimes you would go in behind another customer and there would be nobody there except just this girl because the other customer would be away in the back with Mr. Melchizedek—his name was—buying boxes of cigars.

G

It might be a prosperous business type or it might be under-grads—not the scholarship ones idling on your taxes, since their money didn't run quite to *that*. The really wealthy ones, as you could tell at once.

Come to think of it he might have said to this girl, *A five-shilling cigar*. Only perhaps you don't say just that. There was this Ginger Grant from Glasgow got a girl said she was a secretary, so Ginger took her to a restaurant full of executives and said he wanted a bottle of Wee St. George. Only he'd picked it up wrong and the word was French like the words for wines are. *Nuits* it was, meaning some place in France, and the girl laughed at him, which served him right for being so pitiful.

As for this girl in the fag-shop, probably she wasn't bad. In less expensive fag-shops a girl got credit for being ready with a bit of come-hither or cheek. But he'd been in here often enough to see that Mr. Melchizedek—that was his name—discouraged the free-and-easy. Cold-and-lofty was what he approved, as if his girls didn't think much of anything short of selling Sobranies to royal dukes. Phil had seen it work, though. As the girls did thêir stuff he'd seen customers changing their minds and asking for something a bit more expensive than they'd intended. Yes, pitiful people are.

'What about a gold cigarette-case?' the young woman went on.

This time Phil grinned at her. He guessed it was his hair. The way it tumbled about his head cost him eight shillings a week, but there was always a chance of its paying off like now. He felt suddenly more secure. He stopped feeling like there was something wrong with his right buttock, where the news-paper was still in his hip-pocket that he'd checked and checked with.

He picked up the sixpence.

'Bottom of the packet,' he said, looking at it. 'Chips and vinegar for one. We'll have to get together another time.'

The young woman sniffed and went frozen up again. The lady, he thought—and he was grinning to himself now, because he liked language—had reassumed her professional manner. Because this customer had come in.

The customer was Phil's own age. His hair was short and

brushed down, with no oil on it. He was tall and fair and free from pimples, as if he bought health soaps and things a lot. He was togged in the more casual sort of clothes for riding a horse in, and he had a flowery affair like a woman's scarf arranged where a man would wear a good American tie. You could see at once he'd come in to do a bit of creating. But in an easy confident way. Graceful nonchalance of the aristocracy.

'I say!' The newcomer spoke almost before the bell had stopped ringing on the door. 'It's absolutely too bad. Is your manager in? Tell him it's Sir Aubrey Moore.'

Phil winked at the young woman but she ignored him. Before she could speak there was the scraping of a hastily moved chair in the back shop. Then in came this oldish silky man with a nasty gliding action like he was on a belt and not on legs. Mr. Melchizedek of course. Phil lingered. He needed his mind taken off things. It was queer that he did, but Christ hé did.

'*Good* afternoon, sir. I 'opes that you are receiving hevry satisfaction, sir.'

Mr. Melchizedek was softly rubbing his hands together, in the way they always make his toady-sort do on the telly. He was a foreigner of course, and his aiches didn't seem to behave in an honest way—not either in one honest way or the other. Phil registered this at once. You can't be a Tombs in Oxfordshire, any more than you can be a Timms or a Belcher or a Pratley, and not be very aware of how foreigners and aliens come seeping in. Like how Radiators and Pressed Steel and Lucys have them from all over, and now blacks, very decent chaps, on the buses.

'It's this mixture you make up for me, you know. My personal mixture, dash it. And it's as dry as dust.' Sir Aubrey Moore tossed an open tobacco-pouch on the counter. It hadn't a coat of arms or even a monogram but it looked expensive. 'Just take a glance at the stuff.'

Phil wondered whether he could toss down any rejected article just like that. It was tossing, all right. Only there was more to it than that. The chap had it so that he could be insolent without being not polite. Phil, whom the laws of electricity were training to get things accurate, had just graphed the young man's manner like this when he saw that 89

Mr. Melchizedek wasn't worried. Mr. Melchizedek was fingering a pinch of the tobacco, and over his pasty face there was coming a kind of pitying but respectful smile.

'No,' Mr. Melchizedek said. 'No, sir—I think not.' He looked up at the young man and gently shook his head. You realized that he had nicely dressed silver hair, so fine that it stirred gently in the breeze of his own soft movements. He might have been the old family butler, remembering how he'd dandled the infant baronet or whatever he was on his knee, and putting him right now on some silly thing he'd said about the old crusted port or the champagne.

'I venture to suggest, sir,' Mr. Melchizedek said, 'that you 'ave neglected one factor, sir. A very simple and very himportant factor if I may say so, sir. The 'igher class of tobaccos, sir, 'as the moisture scientifically hextracted from them.' Mr. Melchizedek closed the pouch and handed it gently back to Sir Aubrey. 'A great pleasure, sir. A great pleasure to be of service at any time, sir. Thank *you*, sir. Good afternoon, sir.'

Phil didn't look at the young man. It didn't seem fair. But he tried another wink at the girl. This time, he thought, she'd have done a snort of laughter if she hadn't been scared of Melchizedek. So Phil put one hand into the front pocket of his jeans—for her benefit, that was—and with the other swung open the door and went out. Male and arrogant, he thought. And he crossed Carfax and walked up Cornmarket Street.

There had been a big bell jangling for some reason in one of the colleges. But here the noise of traffic drowned anything of the sort at once. It was plain these places weren't what they had been when there was nothing but Varsity around. You could see that old Oxford set-up in the plans, enlarged to the size of murals, that Woolworth's decorated their side windows with. He'd thought of going into Marks and Sparks, but now he thought he'd go across and into Woolworth's. There was nothing he wanted to buy but he'd walk round. It was the biggest Woolworth's in the country, they said, and hadn't *he* to think big? He went across.

It was clever. It was clever the way the covered part, before you came to the doors, half sucked you in under the bright lights, specially if it was wet. And those great squashy letters

WOOLWORTH must be psychology; they must be that as they certainly weren't art. He went in.

Phil Tombs passed where the kids got ice-cream and threaded through the idle-buy counters near the doors which were psychology too. He'd go down to Electrical Appliances, where he had professional standing so to speak, and see if there was anything new. The whole place was pretty full. It was all on one floor, all except the cafeteria, and he wondered about the ventilation which was O.K. He wondered what went on on the floors above. Executives in offices, he supposed, some of them smoking Melchizedek's cigars. It must be better fun for a girl working here than in Melchizedek's— except that here you were right out in the open, with customers all round you. It's psychology that it's good to have a wall to put your back to, they say.

He stood still, so that women with parcels and women with children bumped into him, and a man carrying some doubled-up metal curtain-rod pretty well jabbed him in the neck. He was trying what it would be like to be one of these girls—in a sort of pen with these little trays all round, and beyond that always people fingering things or waving ten-bob notes at you. He turned round as if he was facing customers, and then turned round again, so that people must have thought he was cracked. Then it occurred to him that a store detective might come along and be suspecting him. So he hurried on. He didn't know what it was that sometimes made him do these fool things.

He never got to Electrical Appliances, because he stopped again, and this time it was without really knowing it. It was all these people, and all these things—small cheap things mostly, in all these trays and on all these shelves. And there were all the other Woolworth's, and Marks and Sparks all over the place, and Littlewood's, and Great Universal Stores, and the people that used to be the Fifty Shilling Tailors, and the Elegance Taste Economy people and you couldn't say what. There was so much of it all and of everybody—the same sort of people buying the same sort of things and covering up the same sort of bodies with them or fixing them up on Sunday afternoons in the same sort of houses—that it could only be meaningless. He felt unaccountably scared. So he had to hurry out of Woolworth's, as if suddenly he'd been told he didn't belong there. And perhaps no more you do, he thought. The place could belong to you now, in a manner of speaking. So you no longer belong to it. Write your bleeding autobiography, and call it *Outside Woolworth's*. A good title. But perhaps it wouldn't be a very good book.

Outside Woolworth's there was a newspaper woman and posters. Phil went past keeping his glance away. It was like hunted-man stuff. You stop at a corner, with the collar of a stolen coat up round your mouth, and there suddenly is this poster with a photograph of you. A corner of it gets loose and flaps in the wind. A few fallen leaves scurry by. Then a bit of old newspaper blows across the street, catches on the poster, blots out the photograph just as a dick or some nosey old woman might be glancing at you and then turning to look at it. You pull the collar higher and hurry on. And the wind is icy in the streets and you haven't got the price of a cup of coffee left.

Phil turned into George Street. He found his hand was still in that front pocket, like he'd put it in a bit of sexy swagger for Melchizedek's girl. It was clutching his sixpence change. The last sixpence of his old life. Through the thin lining, close to where his tight-fitting X Fronts left off, he rasped the milled edge of the coin against his groin. *Face* it, he said to himself. *Begin to think it out. About Beryl, for instance, and all that.*

Instead of thinking, he looked around, that being easier. It was getting on for six, the time in Oxford you begin to get what some book calls the two nations in the streets. Of course you get them all day: always those undergrads and their professors; always plenty of town folk—women in from Cowley and the housing estates shopping, clerks hurrying importantly around to hand each other bits of paper. But it's in the evening you get this split-up affair of young men: the undergrads again, in twos mostly and smiling and talking rapidly; lads from Morrises and that, more in fours and sixes, laughing and shouting like they were paid for it, sweeping the pavements line-abreast where there are no dicks about. Fancying themselves regular Teds, a lot of them, but not much good at it and through with it in eighteen months. They have girls after that and don't come much to the centre of the city, a part inconvenient for what they're mostly thinking about. Another eighteen months and somebody's got careless, so that it's all waiting for a house and doing crazy sums about the never-never. Sort of so many Ages of Man, and that's several blewed before you notice. Of course in the electrical trades you're a bit apart from it; you have your standards. Still, he'd done that Ted stuff himself a bit before latching on to Beryl. And for some reason he'd dressed a bit young this evening. The word was nostalgia, he told himself.

Suddenly he knew he was hungry. He'd better have something before he went home—since what he'd have to face *there* there was no telling. Hour of destiny, perhaps. Facing it at least for a minute *now*, and therefore a bit absent about what he was doing, he went into this Pompadour. Never been there before. He could see at once it was cheap. He could see it was rather an undergrad place. Didn't matter, of course. He sat down at the counter and ordered something from a man in a tall white cap affair. Pretending to be a chef.

Phil didn't know why he did it, and it must have been just because he was disturbed. But as the man turned away, Phil made some fool gesture above his own head.

'Pitiful,' he said.

'Pitiful,' a voice agreed in his ear. And it added something quite unintelligible.

'What's that?' Phil turned and stared.

'*Cucullus non facit monachum*,' repeated the voice.

Phil noticed the repetition wasn't quite confident. It was rather as if the speaker felt he might have got one of his words wrong.

'Come again,' Phil said. The speaker's being an undergrad made him use this cheap Yank challenge.

'The cowl, or whatever it is, doesn't make the monk. And that affair doesn't make the chap able to cook.'

Phil took a quick, shy look at the person on the next stool. It was another young man of his own age, just as it had been in Melchizedek's. This one had dark hair cut in a straight fringe just above his eyebrows like a kid's. He was wearing cavalry twills and a draught-board jersey with a neck that came right up round his chin. He was looking at Phil a bit shyly in turn. Talking that Latin, or whatever it was, he must have been taking Phil for an undergrad. But he couldn't think that for long.

'It's a soft job,' Phil said contemptuously. 'Slapping out fish and slush.'

'No, it isn't.' The young man spoke with an air of authority. 'Not among all those ovens and hot plates on a sticky day. No fun at all.'

The young man said 'fun' like it might rhyme with 'Goon' in 'Goon Show'. So Phil knew at once that this wasn't a public schoolboy. He was one of the ones that was at the varsity on that bleeding PAYE, all right. Grammar School after the Eleven-Plus, and stayed there, and then everything paid out of what was missing from his, Phil Tombs's, pay packet. At the end of the Varsity term, likely enough, he'd return to Nottingham or Leeds to a home very like Phil's own.

This discovery didn't in itself at all make Phil take to his neighbour. If he had to choose a companion to live on a desert island with, he thought, he'd as soon have Sir Aubrey What-had-his-name-been as a jumped-up kid out of his own class. On the other hand, Phil had rather liked being casually addressed, even in gibberish, by an undergrad. Here they were, side by side, and a bit of talk was only sensible. Phil, who liked things to make sense, and who suspected that he was soon to be at grips with things that somehow didn't, felt he should manage a civil reply.

'What d'you think he pulls in—him with the white cap?' he asked.

'Ten pounds. That, and a bit of overtime. I know, because I've done it myself.

'Done it yourself?' Phil was puzzled. 'Before becoming an undergrad?'

'No. Last Long Vac.'

'Last long what?'

'In the holidays—the university holidays. It helped a bit at home. And, after that, I had £30 left to get to Italy on.'

Remembering Cyprus, yet aware of unknown worlds, Phil asked truculently:

'What did you want to be going to Italy for?'

'It must have been to further my education. At least, I got an extra £15 from my college's travel fund on that assumption.' The young man seemed to reflect that Phil mightn't make much of this note. 'I loved Italy,' he said. 'And it's very queer, you know—seeing so many staggeringly beautiful things which one already has a notion of from pictures.'

'I can't say *I've* ever seen Italian pictures like that.' Phil glanced at the young man, and was aware of misunderstanding. 'Nothing but slums and starvation and thievery in the pictures that have come *my* way. But bleeding well-made, some of them.'

'Of course, the poverty's frightful.' Phil could see that the young man was anxious to deny taking only an arty view of the Wops and their country. 'Particularly in the south. And they say Sicily's worst of all. Did you hear Danilo Dolci?'

'Dolci?' Phil was mystified by what appeared to be an abrupt change of subject. 'Would he be one of those crooners in Saturday Club?'

'No, he's nothing like that.' The young man flushed under his kid's fringe, just as if he felt it had been him and not Phil who had said something silly. 'A chap who's done astonishing things among absolutely destitute people there in Sicily. He was talking about it in the Town Hall not long ago.'

'Never heard of him, I'm sure.' Phil accompanied these ungracious words with a carefully uncouth gesture to the man in the white cap, who responded by slapping him out another portion of sausage and tomato. Then he realized that he had no honest impulse to act tough. 'I'll bet,' he said, jerking a thumb towards the white-capped man, '*he* doesn't spend his ten quid on going off to Italy. Still, that was quite an idea of yours. The Leaning Tower and the Pope and the Lido, all done on fish and slosh.' He found himself giving his new acquaintance a friendly grin. 'Not that ten quid's much for a week's work. We get that during strikes for no work at all.'

'Cowley?'

'Uhuh. But I'm getting out. Telecommunications for me.' Phil hesitated, remembering that this was perhaps no longer true. 'After finishing some exams at the 'Tec,' he added doggedly.

'You said ten pounds?' The young man was staring at Tombs in honest respect. 'You don't mean that strike benefit—?'

'Strike benefit my foot. We get a flat ten quid from the bosses when we're laid off because there's a strike in Birmingham, and the blokes in Birmingham get a flat ten quid from the bosses when there's a strike here in Oxford. See? Seems to be the way we're fixing it, since that bleeding General Election.'

The young man with the fringe suddenly banged the formica-topped, coffee-slopped counter in front of him. The action startled Phil quite a bit.

'But don't you see,' the young man demanded, 'that Labour lost the Election because that was the way everyone was thinking to fix it already? Putting their shirt on industrial action and the hope of another ten bob a week? And letting political action, which is the only ultimately effective weapon, go to the devil?'

'I don't take much stock of all that.' Phil changed his friendly grin to an expression which he intended to be contemptuous. 'Never been uppety, I haven't. Never been paid, like you lot, to spend all day with the weight off my feet, nosing through books.'

The young man appeared to consider how best to take this. It was obviously to give himself time to think that he ordered a cup of tea. He didn't—not in a place like this, he didn't—secure service as rapidly as Phil did.

'Probably you were cheated of it,' the young man said. 'Education, I mean. The bloody fraud of the Opportunity State. Cheated just as blatantly as if the Prime Minister himself had slunk up and pickpocketed your last sixpence.'

'Had done *what*?' Phil felt a sudden horrid sinking inside. He stared at his second portion of sausage and tomato. He'd been crazy. A last sixpence was precisely what he had—and it wouldn't pay for half the first plateful, let alone this one.

'The whole educational ladder's weighted against the—working-class child.' The young man had hesitated, and Phil thought it was perhaps because he was thinking that ladders aren't things you weight against a chap. But no—it was because the words 'working-class child' had worried him.

Self-conscious about it, you might say.

'Rotten primary schools,' the young man went on. 'Rotten old text-books. Parents hostile or indifferent to the whole idea of grammar school. And the struggle goes on like the ten little niggers. Sixteen working-class children out of a hundred pass the Eleven-Plus. But only one of those gets as far as the university.'

'Two,' Phil said—and at once felt better about his approaching moment of bankruptcy. You can't work with electricity without respecting figures.

'All right, two. The point is that *you* might have been a little nigger later on, just because of some rotten unfairness or another, even if you *had* passed your Eleven-Plus.'

Phil laughed—so loudly that the girl behind the tea-urn stared at him in cold disapproval. Recklessly he waved at her to give him a cup.

'*That!*' he said. 'You couldn't *not* pass that if you was paid for it. And as for hostile parents, my uncle made me take extra lessons for the flipping thing from an old wife down our street. And passed it in spite of her, I did.'

'Then you *were* at a grammar school?' The young man asked this with inoffensive surprise. The grammar, he was clearly thinking, hadn't stuck.

'Christ, I was. And out again as quickly as I could get them to put a boot in my bottom, man. Took a look at Latin and all that, and just knew I had to go either technical or cracked. Yes, I'd have been psychological by the time I was eighteen if I hadn't got out of it.'

'It must have taken a bit of nerve.' From under the black fringe the young man was again looking at Phil respectfully. 'But you're lucky, probably. You'll make more money out of your telecommunications than I'll ever do after reading P.P.E.'

'What's that mean?'

'Philosophy, Politics, and Economics.'

'I see.' Phil noticed the lack of any edge, this time, to his own voice. Suddenly, he was feeling rather depressed. It was as if he'd been sitting drinking beer for a long time, and not this stuff meant to taste like char. 'You at one of these colleges?' he asked abruptly, although he knew perfectly well that the young man was. 'Know a friend of mine, name of Sir Aubrey Moore?'

'Aubrey Moore?' The young man turned towards Phil, so that the fringe parted like a theatre-curtain above his nose. 'I know him by sight. He's at my college. But I've never spoken to him. He's a most frightful bloody.'

For a moment Phil was puzzled. Then he understood. 'Do you mean,' he asked, 'Two Nations—that sort of thing? Even inside your bleeding college?'

'Four, I'd say.' The young man had flushed slightly, almost like he was a teacher starting to give the kids a talk on sex. 'Etonians, for a start. And perhaps Wykehamists. Then all the people from all the other public schools.'

'That's two? Wouldn't it be a bit a matter of dads and so on, as well as schools?'

'Yes, of course. There are cross-currents one would never get to understand, even if one wanted to. But, roughly, that's two. And then there are two quite distinct lots from grammar schools. And it's nothing *but* dads, this time. White-collar dads—the lower-middle class, in fact. And then plain proletarian dads, like mine who's a coalminer.'

'I see,' Phil, having an inquiring mind, found this interesting. It wasn't, on the other hand, very important. At least it wouldn't be, except for this odd thing that was due to happen.

'That about this Moore being a friend of mine,' he said. 'It was only a crack, of course.'

'Well, that was the explanation that did just cross my mind.' The young man with the fringe smiled briefly—it was something he didn't often do—and then looked serious again. 'My name's Peter Sharples,' he said hurriedly.

'Mine's Phil Tombs.'

Phil said this and waited. There were those who said 'Work in the cemetery, I suppose?' like they were asking for one on the clock. And there were those who refrained.

'Pitiful tea they do you here,' Sharples said.

This Pompadour was filling up so that you began to think there was something wrong with your elbows. There was a narrow shelf along one wall, and these pillars with shelves round them, and stools so narrow you felt you were perching on the end of a pole. But mostly people stood about, and he'd been wrong about its being chiefly undergrads. In the centre it was Teds and some girls lounging round, like the place was a straight coffee-bar juke-box joint down St. Ebbe's. But there was a group of Wops over by the Espresso, and if the crush went on like this they'd soon be able to get around to pinching the girls' behinds, which is a Wop's chief idea of fun. And there were five or six Yanks off an airfield, crew-cut and drinking cokes like kids, only it wasn't much like kids that their eyes went up and down when there was a girl to be let know that their eyes were going up and down *her*. It was hot and airless in here and there were a lot of smells around, and when Phil looked at these three plastic oranges they always have churning round under glass on the surface of the orange squash he almost felt giddy for a moment and he wasn't sure that they didn't suggest something. But now he looked at the undergrad Peter Sharples who had said nothing about filling tombs. Then he surprised himself by the question he asked Peter Sharples straight out.

'What would you do,' Phil asked—and because he'd finished his char he was rasping that sixpence in his groin again—'with twenty thousand pounds?'

'That's an easy one,' Sharples said, and got out a packet of cigarettes. 'Smoke?'

'Thanks.' Phil took a cigarette. They were common fags, and he somehow didn't feel like bringing out his Camels and suggesting an exchange. Once he had read a book called *Inside Oxford* or something like that, so he wasn't surprised that Sharples wasn't surprised by his question. He knew that the undergrads sit up all night asking each other questions and usually nothing personal involved. Taught to exercise unsleeping intellectual curiosity was what the book had said. He'd rather be taught telecommunications himself, but he saw the idea—which was something he hadn't been sure the man who wrote the book had. Perhaps if you had a real line on unsleeping intellectual curiosity yourself you didn't write books with names like *Inside Oxford*. But now Sharples was answering him.

'Twenty thousand?' Sharples said. 'I'd be an M.P. before I was in my thirties.'

'But what would you *do* with it?'

'Invest it, of course. I could invest it perfectly safely so that it would bring in a thousand a year. Then I could afford to take a job on low pay on the Labour Party Research Unit, and begin nursing a constituency as well.'

'How d'you know you'd get a constituency?'

'I'm not a moron, Phil. I'll quite possibly get a First in Schools. And a thousand a year would be just the job after that. Bless their egalitarian hearts. They'd jump at me.'

Not all of this speech was meaningful to Phil Tombs, who was much struck, however, by the casual way in which he had been called Phil.

'You a socialist, Peter?' he asked. 'Would you still be a socialist if you had that twenty thousand?'

'Of course I should—and a much more effective one at that.'

'You don't think a lot of money is likely to change a man?'

'If he's any good, he'll use it to change himself the way he *wants* to change himself. Of course there would be pitfalls. But I don't think twenty thousand is enough to bring you much in the way of the really serious ones.'

'Not *enough*?' Phil made an effort to get hold of this point of view. It was a matter of orders of magnitude. 'As for what?' he demanded. Out of the corner of his eye he saw that the man in the white cap was making out a bill.

'Well, a life of dissipation, for instance. A thousand a year wouldn't take you far on that.'

'Happen not.' Phil picked up the bill, looked at it with a great air of casual interest, and dropped it again. 'But you could have a pretty hot year or two if you blewed the whole capital.'

'Is that what you'd do?' Peter Sharples did now seem to be a little wondering what this was in aid of. And he had paid his own bill. Farther down the counter, the man in the white cap was pretty well driving a couple of lingering customers from their stools. There wasn't long to go. Phil put his hand up to his collar and tugged at it like he was in pain. 'What would I?' he asked with some genuine inattentiveness. 'Search me if I blamed well know.' He gave another tug, and then contrived to sway alarmingly on his stool. 'Bleeding hot in here.' He glanced behind him, being anxious to see whether the Pompadour kept much in the way of staff on this side of the counter. There really was a terrific crush. 'No bleeding air.' He did a rapid rocking movement this time, first bumping into Peter Sharples's shoulder and then into a hunched-up man who was noisily eating soup on his other side. He raised his voice to a pitch at which there was no chance of its being neglected. 'Believe,' he said loudly, 'I'm going to pass out.'

'Easy with your shoving, there.' The hunched-up man had straightened himself and turned indignantly towards Phil, soup dribbling down his chin. Then his expression changed. 'You going to be sick?' he said.

This was better than could have been hoped for. Phil gave a retch and this time pitched straight forward. Everybody immediately round about was aware of him now, and he became the subject of a widening circle of comment.

'Chap passed out.'

'Young chap puking all over the counter.'

'Not surprised . . . worse'n a submarine . . . anyone would faint.'

''Ere, I can't see. Lemme look.'

'Eaten their bloody prawns, I expect. Fatal this time of year. . . . Stop shoving, can't you?'

'Now then, order please.' The man with the white cap was leaning angrily over the counter. 'Let him have a bit of air, can't you?'

At this Phil lifted his head rapidly.

'Air!' he said loudly, and dropped it again.

'You're his friend, aren't you?' The man in the white cap addressed Peter Sharples challengingly. 'Get him to the door, for Christ's sake, before he really is sick. He's only groggy. Get him on his feet, can't you? How often have I told the boss the ventilation here's a disgrace? Take him out and let him breathe a bit. Gangway there, please. No crowding. Nothing but a patron slightly indisposed.'

The indisposed patron was already on his feet and—although leaning picturesquely on the arm of his friend—making pretty good speed for fresh air. The crowd in the Pompadour parted, gaped curiously, and closed up again.

For a moment Phil's head positively lolled on Sharples's shoulder.

'Peter,' he hissed, 'when we're out—*run*!'

And they ran—Phil because that was the extravagant plan that had come to him, Sharples because simple manhood would admit of nothing else. There were a few angry shouts as they pelted down George Street. These didn't matter at all. And then, very disconcertingly, there was a blast on what could only be a policeman's whistle. Shoulder to shoulder, they ran on panting. Once they glanced sideways at each other, excited and very scared. They were back in the same sort of childhood, a childhood in which there had been much bolting from coppers who were commonly imaginary but sometimes real, and in which awesome talk went round of borstals and remand homes and what happened if they got you there.

They parted very casual, Phil and Peter, outside the gaol, since they had swung round that way after running to the end of New Inn Hall Street. It looked as if the copper hadn't blown his whistle after them at all, but perhaps just after some fool motorist crashing the lights up by what Peter called the Corn. Imaginary coppers right enough, Peter said, just like when he and his gang had used to be raiding the condemned back-to-backs behind the Gas Works for the waste-pipes in the kitchen sinks.

Better part outside the gaol than inside, Phil said. But, although they both laughed like anything, a man could have told they were surprised with themselves—Phil because he'd never done this sort of thing before, only heard of it or sometimes watched it, and Peter because it was like something in the library catalogue, Memories of My Dead Life. And Phil had done it because he was excited and it looked as if he was upset about this thing he hadn't let on about, and Peter had done it because they'd been pals for outside of a half-hour or so.

Only Peter Sharples, of course, had paid his bill. And now he said a queer thing.

'What'll you do?' he said, still flushed and laughing. 'Send them a P.O.?'

Just for the moment, Phil thought he was adding a bit to

the joke. But no, Peter meant it—which to Phil's mind was to ditch the joke altogether. And Phil ought to have gone straight to that vocabulary he kept and fished out something about the creeping paralysis of bourgeois morality. That would have been a good one. But all he managed was to say 'Well, p'raps' awkwardly and unconvincingly, and this had the effect of making their parting a bit flat. He thought of saying careless, 'What's that college of yours call itself?' but it turned out he didn't care to. Anyway, there'd be something in the Reference Library that gave the names of all the undergrads and their colleges, if he ever wanted to get on to this Peter Sharples again. So he said 'So long' like it might be to a man in the next street. Only, fifteen yards on he turned his head and gave a wave, and he gave a grin too that said they'd had a bit of fun all right.

From *The Man Who Won the Pools* by J. I. M. Stewart

Typical Working Class?

An analysis of the character of the much-admired Andy Capp might be of some service to the politicians and social workers who spend so much of their time in endeavouring to understand what makes the ordinary English working man tick.

Andy Capp puts little into life. He hates work (8 cartoons), is lazy (20), greedy (8), avoids paying his rent (5) and other debts (3), vain (2), selfish (4) and uncouth (8). He is an ill-mannered guest (3) and worse-mannered host (12).

He gets as much out of life as he can. More often than not he has a cigarette in his mouth (345) or at any rate to hand (17). He visits the pub regularly (65) and, while he sometimes gets drunk (30), has a strict code of pub ethics which includes: always make sure the other fellow buys his round (2), and never let anyone else drink your beer (2).

H

Drink means more to him than practically anything else (14). He likes a drink at home, too (20).

He is a keen sports fan. He plays soccer (21), snooker (12), cards (8), darts (6), the pools (5) and cricket (4). He further enjoys fishing (1) and running (1), and is addicted to pigeons (4). As a spectator he goes to soccer matches (16), greyhounds (4) and horse-racing (1). He is a bad loser (13) and has been known to become violent both when playing (7) and watching (4).

His home life revolves around his wife Florrie, in a relationship not always sunny. He is constantly yelling at her (17), refusing her simple pleasures (10) such as new hats (2) and outings (2), keeps her up late when he is out drinking (3) and loathes her family (3). He pretends to give her help when doing nothing of the sort (13), idles while she toils (18), cadges from her (4) and is callous about her (5).

Fairly frequently he lifts his hands to her (16), knocking her down (4), throwing her out of the house (3), knocking her about (1), throwing a bottle at her (1), pushing a paintbrush at her face (1), throwing her on to the bed (1) or off the couch (1), throttling her (1), throwing a snowball at her (1), putting her in the dustbin (1), throwing the flat-iron at her (1). When it isn't hands, it is feet: he kicks her out of bed (1), or on the behind (2).

Now and then she gets her own back, insulting him both in his hearing (12) and out of it (8), finding ways of getting back at him (3), fooling him (2), getting her own way (2) and very occasionally hitting him with what lies to hand (3). Sometimes it all becomes too much for them both, and either she leaves him (5) or he—Capp is cynical about marriage (3)—leaves her. They both always come back.

It is all reprehensible, shocking, uncouth. Andy sets an appalling example to the youth of Britain. But Mr. Capp is irresistible.

From *At Your Peril* by Hugh Cudlipp,
joint managing director of the *Mirror* Group.

Manners Maketh Man

Nowadays people who wish to move up in the world can attend evening classes in 'Gracious Living'. Books on etiquette find a ready sale. Here is some advice from one of them:

An etiquette book, like a dictionary, should be available in every home as a ready reference when one is in doubt about customs and manners. Everyone should read a book of etiquette for himself without depending on another person to answer his questions. Everyone should know and practise the fundamentals of good manners, for one's conduct is largely responsible for the place one holds in the world.

Etiquette books are written to help people to have a good time; not to hinder them. They contain information about good manners which should make life easier for all those who wish to learn it. Rules regarding good manners are like the laws of the land—they are written for the benefit of its citizens. The citizen who obeys them is always respected.

Books on good manners have been in circulation farther back than any of us can remember, and yet no book on etiquette has ever been written that has pleased everyone. We see things in all of them we'd like to change; but no authority can afford to make a drastic change, for our present-day customs represent the best of the conventions endorsed by fine old families from the beginning of our own modern times. These families were not of 'special kind' or segregated by any means, but were families who respected the rights of others first. After a while a pattern of conduct was formed which is a good one for all of us to follow. Some of these patterns cannot be changed; no more than the true architecture of a house can be changed. Slight variations can be made in a pattern of conduct, just as a house can be remodelled; but nothing of intrinsic value in either should be discarded. Our first writers on etiquette used for their authority the manners of the old royal courts, with few changes. Later authorities have pronounced changes in conventions to meet the wishes of the times, and the people.

The author of these pages allows a change at any time the

situation demands it. Sometimes doing a thing in what seems a more sensible way is showing better judgement than following the regular accepted way.

A few variations of small degree are made in almost any house. Customs in a household depend upon the architecture of the house, the number of servants, the size or location of the establishment, or the tradition of family custom. Therefore, no one should criticise a well-managed house which disregards services or habits which are customary in other houses. If the details of recognised conventions cannot be carried out, one should not feel disgruntled, but accept the circumstances with tolerance.

The author has attempted to make this volume useful by writing in a concise style. This style makes rapid reading possible and should encourage busy people to read. Great care and effort have gone into the work so that it may be simple and easy to remember. If one has not been taught to cultivate consideration of others, one might as well have neglected to learn one's reading, writing and arithmetic. Etiquette is education, and without its basic principles no man succeeds.

This book gives the accepted ways of meeting the problems in present-day good manners. Its object is to guide those interested in learning the best social customs. It was written for busy people and for those who prefer an inexpensive book on the etiquette which the average person needs to know. By reading the contents carefully and thoughtfully, one should be prepared to face confidently and in an unembarrassed way any situation requiring a knowledge of social conventions.

DINING-ROOM AND RESTAURANT CUSTOMS
(1) *What is meant by 'Table d'hôte' on a menu?*
ANS: 'Table d'hôte' means a fixed price for the meal, regardless of how much or how little one orders.
(2) *What is meant by 'A la carte' on a menu?*
ANS: 'A la carte' means that each dish is paid for as listed on the menu.
(3) *Should a woman leave her wraps at the cloakroom or take them with her into the restaurant?*

ANS: She keeps her coat and hat with her. A man leaves his in the cloakroom.

(4) *Is it correct for a woman to select the table in a restaurant?*
ANS: Yes, she may tell the man her preference, and he of course tells the head waiter, or leads the way to the table. The woman is given the place facing the street, or the place overlooking the best scenery.

(5) *May one change one's table from that indicated by the head waiter?*
ANS: Yes, if it is done quietly.

(6) *Does a gentleman seat a lady, or does he allow the waiter to do so?*
ANS: The waiter seats the lady if he is well trained; otherwise, the gentleman does.

(7) *Who orders the meal, the man or the woman?*
ANS: Usually the man orders, but consults the woman as to her preferences.

(8) *When in doubt how should one select silver at a dinner?*
ANS: Watch the hostess and use the silver according to her example. One usually finds that silver is laid in the order in which it is to be used according to courses. The first to be used is farthest from the plate, and the last nearest to the plate.

(9) *When one is using the knife and fork to cut meat how should the fork be held?*
ANS: The fork should be held with the prongs down and with the forefinger resting on the back of the lower end of the handle.

(10) *Is it correct to leave a spoon in a tea-glass or a coffee-cup while eating?*
ANS: Never; the spoon should always be taken out and put into the saucer.

(11) *May a salad be cut with a knife?*
ANS: Yes, if it is a lettuce salad. A fork should be sufficient for other salads.

(12) *Is it necessary to eat a little of all food that is served at a dinner in a restaurant or at a first-class hotel when you are sure that something on the menu does not agree with you?*
ANS: Certainly not. To do so would be putting good manners before health.

(13) *How should you eat olives?*

ANS: Hold them in your fingers one at a time, and take small bites.

(14) *When eating at a table is it correct to hold a sandwich in one's hand until it is finished?*

ANS: No! To put the sandwich on one's plate and pick it up again is better.

(15) *How should the cutlery be left after one has finished eating?*

ANS: As a rule the cutlery that has been used should be laid on the plate and the unused pieces should be left on the table.

(16) *Is it correct to smoke at the table?*

ANS: Yes, if the hostess has suggested it; otherwise ask the hostess if she objects.

(17) *What does a guest do with the napkin at the end of a meal?*

ANS: He leaves it unfolded on the table beside his plate.

(18) *What amount should a waiter be tipped?*

ANS: Ordinarily the waiter receives ten per cent of the bill.

(19) *Does one tip the head waiter?*

ANS: No, unless he has performed some special service.

(20) *How should one leave a chair at the table of a dining-room or of a restaurant?*

ANS: One should push the chair under the table rather than leave it out from the table.

(21) *Is it correct to look at the bill before paying it?*

ANS: To glance over a bill to see if any mistakes are made is correct, but a detailed examination is unforgivable.

(22) *If some unforeseen circumstance arises after an acceptance to an invitation has been given, is it correct to decline?*

ANS: Yes, if one gives reasons which are good ones.

(23) *Is it correct for one to put his elbows on the table while eating?*

ANS: No! The left hand, except when both hands are needed to manage the knife and fork, should be kept in one's lap during the meal. However, if there is plenty of room at the table, one may rest one's arms on the table between courses.

(24) *Is it permissible when all tables in a crowded restaurant are in use to ask strangers if one may sit with them?*

ANS: Yes, no person or even two people should be so selfish as to occupy more space than is necessary for their own comfort. One might say: 'I beg your pardon, but I believe all the tables are in use. May I sit with you?' By all means ask, don't just walk over and sit down.

(25) *Is it impolite to refuse a dish that is passed?*

ANS: To refuse several dishes would be rude, but no hostess should feel offended if a guest should refuse one or two.

(26) *Is it correct to ask for a second helping?*

ANS: If one knows the hostess well, and sees that there is plenty of food, one might ask for a small second helping.

(27) *Is it necessary to wait until the hostess has begun eating before a guest can begin?*

ANS: Certainly not, a guest begins eating when he is served.

(28) *May a guest refuse an alcoholic drink?*

ANS: Certainly, a person may say: 'No thank you, I don't drink.' That is sufficient, and to give a reason is not necessary. When a hostess is serving drinks, she should have soft drinks for those who do not take alcohol.

(29) *When an informal dinner is announced should a guest stand behind his chair at the table until the hostess is ready to sit?*

ANS: Yes, all guests should stand either behind or beside their chairs until the hostess is ready to be seated.

(30) *How may a guest in a restaurant summon a waiter?*

ANS: If there is no wall-button, a person might tap his water-glass lightly with a spoon; by no means whistle, or hiss to a waiter.

A TIP TO THE TIPPERS

There is a legend that back in the early eighteenth century a London innkeeper put a small slotted box on each table with a sign 'To Insure Promptness' and that the word 'tip' was formed from the initial letters of the sign.

From that day to this the custom of tipping has spread until it has reached almost every country of the world. Most countries have permitted the system, while some have adopted it for a trial only and then have abandoned it on the basis that it was unfair to the public. In some European countries direct tipping is discouraged in favour of a service charge plan, whereby ten per cent is added to the guest's bill and paid by the management of the establishment to its servants on the regular pay-day.

Needless to say, tipping is an unnecessary evil and is looked upon by many people as a polite form of blackmail and a racketeer job in disguise. A survey of opinions on tipping made by a popular magazine recently showed that only 23 per cent favoured the system. Even people working in the servant classification deplore the practice, because they can never be assured of definite, sufficient compensation for their services; and, generally speaking, customers are uncomfortable about tipping. Of course, there are some well-trained servants who make enormous sums from tips and would never consent willingly to abolishing them. Substantial fortunes, even, have been built on tips. One head porter of a fashionable hotel in London left £25,000; the head keeper of a baronial estate willed £50,000 to his heirs; one butler to a nobleman left an estate of over £16,000. When these fortunes were being made, wealthy people tipped more lavishly than they do now; occasionally a guest would tip £25, or even £250, for one night's entertainment. Of course, these instances were few and far between, but the facts are recorded.

People tip for different reasons; the majority tip because tipping is customary, even though they abhor it; many tip because they want to appear superior to the persons receiving the money, and still others tip in a spirit of kindness and sympathy for the employee.

However, very few people would extravagantly tip the cloakroom attendant or the receptionist in a fashionable night-club if they knew that the management got the money instead of the dazzling little beauty stationed in a conspicuous place for the purpose of obtaining donations from wealthy patrons. In many places tips are merely dropped into a box for the management, and the attractive girl draws only £4 or £5 for a week's salary. Many times disputes arise among waiters and waitresses when tips are divided. In some cases tipping is on the borderline of commercial bribery, and the public is worked from every angle by a group who pool and split the proceeds. We, that is, most of us, agree that the tipping performance is not ethical and certainly falls short of being thoroughly democratic. Even people of the servant classification refuse to tip freely when they are dining out, or are in positions to tip.

When the subject is analysed, there is little excuse for tipping. Many people have begun to think out this problem for themselves and often ask the question: 'Why should I, one individual, help to pay the servants that the employer is under obligation to pay?' That sounds like straight thinking and valid reasoning. Then, too, we are inclined to believe that if a few exclusive places can operate without the tip system, others could, whether they admit it or not. The only way it will ever be abolished is for the public to stop giving tips; then the employers will begin to pay sufficiently large salaries to their servants.

From *Good Manners in a Nutshell* by Sally Hines

How to remove class distinctions

In Britain in 1960, the majority of middle-class boys and girls, plus those who were trained to become middle-class, were educated up to the age of eighteen or beyond, while their social life was also strenuously organised. By contrast, the majority of working-class boys and girls left school hardly educated at fifteen, to proceed at once into a pseudo-adult life of earning and spending, most of them without membership of any leisure-time organisation.

It is interesting that both the Crowther and the Albemarle Reports emphasised that in the new British society this class contrast was socially harmful and no longer justifiable. It led to an undoubted waste of youthful ability, it led to renewed class distinctions, it engendered youthful malaise and played its part in spreading juvenile delinquency. To lessen this discrepancy, both Reports—and this is the crucial point—proposed State intervention to arrest some of the dangerous trends of the affluent society. The basic recommendation was that the outlook of the country's teenagers should be shaped much more directly through the conscious endeavours of the community and not merely left to the combined persuasions of the advertisers, the Press, and the record industry.

. . . Just as in the mid-fifties there was a 'break-through' in material consumption, so there now has to be a 'break-through' in education, because it is evident that the present secondary modern school system, the system for the seventy to eighty per cent majority, is not adequate in preparing boys and girls for the new society.

There is already an extensive literature on its inadequacies. For present-day needs, the system falls short in that the majority of boys and girls leave too early. A good many of the jobs into which they are drawn are from their nature tedious, mechanical, monotonous, offering little outlet for natural adolescent emotions and so creating a sense of frustration—this phenomenon has been noted in German and American studies as well as in this country. Perhaps much of this emotional frustration during the working day cannot be helped: all the more reason, therefore, for not exposing adolescents to it at the immature age of fifteen.

In the second place, there is a fair measure of agreement among teachers that the secondary modern school system with its present-day curriculum is inadequate as a 'bridge' to working life. The shock when young teenagers encounter the different morality and temptations of working life is often an acute one.

However, to my mind the main defect of the present State school system lies in the way in which it still perpetuates outworn class distinctions. Under the tripartite secondary school structure set up in 1944, by which abler boys and girls are 'creamed off' at eleven, not merely to go to different schools, but, in effect, into a different social life, cultural class distinctions are being preserved and even intensified which are inappropriate to the affluent society. And this is not merely a matter of different education within the school walls. The exaggerated difference in school-leaving age plays an equal part. The authors of the Albemarle Report noted that those teenagers who at fifteen had gone into easy jobs with good money, were spending most of their earnings on a surprisingly narrow range of mass-produced consumption goods and entertainments; for instance, not merely on pop records in general, but each month on a very few records which the industry plugs as top-of-the-month hits. In view of the increasing power and skill of advertising techniques, this need surprise nobody. The trouble is, however, that the whole outlook of such teenagers also becomes shaped and narrowed by the advertisers' culture which is projected at them in order to promote the sale of the products. A working-class girl who is induced to spend a pound a week on pop records and another pound on hairstyling and cosmetics—which is common enough—is through her very preoccupation with this expenditure isolated in class terms from other girls of her age who at grammar school and technical colleges are being taught quite different cultural values.

This excessively class-orientated system of education, whereby the majority of boys and girls are pushed (or lured) far too early into the racket of the teenage market, is harmful in a number of ways. There is little need to stress the waste of abilities among early leavers which is involved. There is, however, one special piece of evidence of a sort of cultural 'downward pull' at work in the affluent society which ought to receive attention.

To judge from the regular complaints of certain teachers, something like a genuine breakdown of discipline has in recent years occurred in a number of the more difficult secondary modern schools in various parts of the country. In most cases, these schools are found in areas like the traffic-filled inner working-class districts of London, where the population tends to be unorganised and shifting and there is little, if any, local community spirit. Often enough, these are also among the schools worst affected by the persistent shortage of teaching staff. But the problem goes further than this. As teachers see it, many boys and girls of thirteen and fourteen in these schools have their minds already so firmly fixed on the world of jobs and money and the glittering attractions of the commercial youth culture that they regard their last years of school as a mere senseless waste of time and react accordingly.

. . . For the schools and the teachers concerned, the problem of such apparently unteachable fourteen-year-olds is today serious enough, but I suspect strongly that the resistance of these particular working-class boys and girls to school is due far less to inbred low intelligence, as is often alleged, than it is a cultural problem; if one likes, a peculiarly English class problem. The resistance seems like a survival of historic class differences, a hangover from past generations of degraded English working-class life, in which these boys and girls still display the defensive hostility of the old slums against a middle-class institution like secondary school. The lure of the crude commercial youth culture, whose standards are so much more easily attained than school knowledge, has now evidently helped to increase this resistance. But, just because I believe the problem posed by these obstructive teenagers to be largely cultural, I also feel that it is one which longer compulsory school attendance, more individual attention in teaching, and a keener sense of purpose in school life could go far to solve, especially in more democratic schools where the natural leaders are not 'creamed off' but are present to set the tone.

From *The Insecure Offenders* by T. R. Fyvel

8 Pop culture

What makes a Great Star? Is it the right record . . . the right backing group . . . the right manager? No. There's only one thing that makes a Great Star, or a Great Group, and that is personality. Proof of this are the Stones (*the Rolling Stones*). They were voted No. 1 Group even before they'd really topped the Hit Parade. Why? The answer is obvious—because they've all got tremendous personalities.

From *Pop Pics Super Greats of '64*

Any music publisher can tell you six months ahead which tune is going to be popular. The public does not make a tune popular. Subject to certain exceptions, some flukes here and there, we know in advance what is going to be popular six months ahead, and the publishing business makes sure a tune it wants to be popular is popular, by spending enough money to make it popular.

A statement by H. Ratcliffe of the Musicians' Union, quoted in *Discrimination and Popular Culture*, edited by Denys Thompson

Once I built a Pop Group

I walked out of the afternoon sun into a wall of brown darkness, blinded by it and feeling like a new boy on his first day in Hell. There was an indefinable noise in the cellar, far off, some kind of orchestrated groan, and apart from that, nothing. I groped for the wall, leaned against it, and waited. After a moment or two, a vast triangle of white shirt-front materialised out of the gloom, shimmered towards me, and stopped. Then a pudgy hand, sticky with what I instantly recognised as spilt booze, felt for mine, and began pumping it methodically. Gradually, I became aware of a face, its outline just discernible in the shirt's iridescence, an inch or so from mine.

'Welcome!' it roared. A sliver of canapé (*a piece of fried bread with anchovies, etc.*) struck me below the left eye. 'Welcome to the Beat Capital of the World!'

'Thank you very much,' I said.

The fat hand slid up to my elbow, and absorbed it, steering me towards a distant oblong glow.

'In what capacity do you come?' asked the shirt. It was a question steeped in ancient mystery, like a sphinx's riddle honed to smoothness on eternity. I was on the point of replying: 'I come from beyond the Mountains of the Moon, O Luminous One, bearing beads and kumquats (*orange-like fruit*), but the voice hadn't finished.

'Not a performer, I imagine, ha-ha-ha?'

'No,' I said. 'A writer.'

'Aha! Lyrics? Librettos, even?'

I explained briefly.

'Salt of the earth,' said the voice, obviously moved. 'Without the gentlemen of the Press, where would any of us be? Delighted you could grace our little, ha-ha, gathering.'

'Thanks for the invitation,' I said.

We arrived at a large, black-painted vault, lit only by a revolving diamantine ball hung above a dance-floor, and the odd electric candle. About fifty people stood around in small fidgeting clumps dropping olive stones and clichés and knocking back free liquor. They all glanced up as I entered, sized me up with what can only be described as a communal sneer, and sank their fangs back into the Veuve-Clicquot.

'It's just a little what-you-might-call a christening party for Beatsville,' murmered the shirt. 'Just a few friends— artistes, A. & R. (*Artists and Repertoire*) men, managers, agents, writers like yourself—people, you know, who feel deeply about the future of beat music. People who want to see this club become a—a Mecca (Ha-ha-ha, don't quote me, can't plug the opposition, eh?) a place where beat music can have a *permanent* home. Drink?'

He propped me against the bar, murmured a silken au revoir and slid off to spread the gospel among the assembled zombies, following a course traceable by tinny giggles and belly-laughs that came straight from the wallet. As he waltzed from guest to guest, I noticed the ranks of immaculate dentures, flashing love. I wondered where all the young people were.

'Been here since half-past bleeding two,' said the man next to me, sourly. He turned, and his Rolleiflex clunked against the Formica. 'They told me there'd be Stones here. Maybe even a Shadow or two. You wouldn't know if there's a Stone coming, by any chance?'

'Sorry,' I said.

'I got eight rolls with me,' said the photographer. 'And me Ikoblitz. I dragged twenty pound of gear all the way from Baker Street. I didn't come here to shoot no pictures of middle-aged bleeding impresarios.' He poured himself a large Scotch, and sank it. 'Trouble with the whole effing pop-scene, my friend, is it's an old man's game. They shove these ten-bob-a-dozen adolescent squealers around like a load of catsmeat, take twenty per cent of the gross, then dump 'em back at the Labour Exchange when the kids get choked off with 'em. Charming!'

A thin, white, stoat-like lad thrust himself between us, towing another teenager behind him.

'Unnerstand you're from Fleet Street,' said the leader. 'You might not've 'eard of Vince yet on account of his first wax not being due till next week. I'd like to present the great new blue beat sensation—Vince Whisper.'

''Ullo,' said Vince. He wouldn't look at me. He just kept staring at his feet, moving them around like thin grey fish at the end of his narrow silk-shining legs. 'Wot paper you from then?'

I told him.

'You said Maureen Cleave,' said Vince to his manager. 'That's who we was going to meet. Maureen Cleave.'

'Vince is five-foot-eight,' said his manager, 'and likes Chinese food and Campari *(a drink)*. He hails from Wood Green, and admires Millie and Chuck Berry. He's not engaged yet, are you, Vince?'

''S'right.'

'What will you do if you make the Top Ten?' I asked.

'He'll buy his family a detached in the suburbs, won't you Vince? And an E-type for himself.'

'Can I 'ave anuvver Coke, Donald?' said Vince.

'Aren't you gonna write all that down?' said Donald.

'I'll remember,' I said.

Three middle-aged entertainers who'd seen service on *Juke Box Jury* edged past, looking as though they were trying to forget, and Donald and Vince took off after them like whippets. A couple of hirsute teenagers in green velvet suits paused in the doorway for effect, a few flashbulbs crackled, and they went away again, yellow hair bobbing.

'Who were they?' I said.

'God knows,' said the photographer. He wound on his film. 'Not my job to sort 'em out. We got a whole bleeding staff for that. Researchers. I just take the pictures, mate.'

At this point, there was a deafening drum-roll, and an answering blaze of white spotlights focused on a stage at the far end of the dance-floor. A tall, bald man in a mauve Shetland sweater and what looked like aluminium jeans called jovially for silence in order to introduce one of the resident groups to whom Beatsville had offered a home, and who were apparently destined to make the Beatles look like Anne Ziegler and Webster Booth. They bounced on to the stage in a faint patter of moist clapping, and, while a hundred narrowed eyes sized them up for growth potential, plugged themselves into a central socket.

'Don't have to sing to be a star these days,' muttered the photographer, 'all you have to do is know how to mend a bleeding fuse.'

The cellar suddenly exploded into a brain-numbing crescendo of electronic din, chord echoing back on chord in a metallic ricochet until any melody that might have stood a chance of escaping disappeared, engulfed by its arrangement. From time to time, a reedy boy-soprano voice poked through a hole in the noise, before going down again.

'I *BOING* you baby, I *KLANGKLANGKLANG* . . . whenever you *BOIYOIYOIYOING* to me-he-he . . . yeah . . .'

The pop-moguls blenched collectively, and began drifting off on a tour of the premises. I tailed after them, to where a dapper little PR man in horn-rimmed glasses and a marcel wave stood waving towards a room hung with baffles and microphones.

'Recording studios,' he explained. 'We believe in centralisation. Kid makes the grade out there, well, we give him the chance to get on to wax RIGHT HERE IN BEATSVILLE! In fact, you might even call this a machine for overnight stardom. Take Thursday—amateur night—kids'll come out of the audience on to the stage, do their numbers, and at the end of the show, the audience'll vote for its favourite group. Prize is a trip backstage and on to a disc *the same evening*. How about that?'

I had a vision of broiler fowls moving bleakly along a conveyor-belt, trussed and ready for polythene embalming, and being shot, half-cooked, on to dinner plates. I slipped away to the men's room. Two middle-aged men, perspiring slightly, were leaning on the towel-machine, arguing about percentages. A conversation was taking place between the occupants of two locked cubicles, about whether the sub-teenage record-buying public was tired of elderly idols and ready for a group it could identify with, a group of, say, twelve-year-olds. Each of them, apparently, knew where he could get his hands on a group like that, right this minute. At a washbasin, a future pop star was being quietly sick, holding a towel up to protect his suède jacket.

'What you writers don't realise,' said a man beside me, who'd obviously been asking a few discreet questions, 'is the coin you can make from the old flip-side giggle. Am I right?'

I said he was.

'A big-name group makes a hit record, see? But they gotta have something on the flip-side, see? Don't have to be nothing special, any old rubbish, just so long as there's a bit of groove on the disc when you turn it over. What people don't realise,' he said, grinning, 'is the writer of the rubbish makes the *exact same royalty* from sales as the bloke what writes the chart-topper. Can't lose.'

He zipped his fly, and felt in his waistcoat for a card.

'You give me a ring in a couple of days,' he said. 'We're crying out for writers. I know all the A. & R. men in the game. Personal friends. Crying out, believe me. That's my speciality, selling flip-sides. All I ask is twenty per cent—can I say fairer than that?'

'I don't think it's my sort of game,' I said.

'You're raving mad,' he said amicably. 'A bright boy like you. You could make a bomb. All you need is a bit of gall, and the right agent. Me, for instance.'

'No talent?' I asked.

'Come on,' he said. 'Be serious, will you?'

An article in 'Punch' by Alan Coren

Fan Mail

These letters appeared in the monthly fan magazine 'The Beatles Book'. The editor is Johnny Dean.

Dear Johnny,

I just had to write and tell you that I (yes me!) have actually met and shook hands with Dear Sweet Ringo's Mum.

I met her in Liddypool at the Beatles one night stand. The show was fantastic, but what really made my night was meeting Mrs. Starkey. She was sitting two rows in front of me, but I met her in the interval in the queue for a place which shall remain nameless! She is gear. (She showed me the lovely watch you bought for her, Ringo.) I also met his cousin and she is also very nice.

Since that night I have not washed my hand!

> Yours with Love,
> Sue Lord (one very grubby fan!)
> (Give a big hug to John from me.)

A Beatles Tragedy

> I knew the dreaded day would come—
> I overheard Dad say to Mum
> 'I'm going to decorate Anne's room.'
> All day I walked round in a gloom.

With sad and heavy heart that night,
I told the Beatles of my plight.
'Dear George and Ringo, John and Paul
I'll have to take you off my wall!'

They looked sad too, as if to say
'We're sorry 'cos we'd like to stay!'
And so I slowly took them down
And tried my hardest not to frown.

At last each wall was stark and bare,
No trace of Beatles anywhere.
Forlorn and sad I crept to bed,
To try to dream of them instead.

I looked around—a sorry sight.
No Beatles there to say goodnight.
I found I could not sleep at all
Without the boys upon my wall.

But now my room's done and I'm glad,
No longer will I feel so sad.
'Cos now they're back upon my wall—
Dear George and Ringo, John and Paul.

                              Anne McDonald

Dear John,

    At 2.31 p.m. today I went to the mailbox and got mail.
As usual, I flipped through the envelopes to see if one of
my Beatle pen-pals had written. I spotted a small brown
letter postmarked 'Liverpool'—Liverpool? That's the
Beatles' home-town—I opened it quickly. My eyes nearly
popped from my head! It was from Mimi Smith—John's
Aunt!! She was thanking me for the drawing I sent. Inside
was enclosed autographs of all the Beatles! I'm still in a fit—
running all over and screaming. But, John, I had to tell you
that I really think your aunt is a really wonderful person.
I can tell from her letter that she's a kind and understanding
woman who loves you very much. You're a lucky man.

                    Sandi Carter (Toronto, Canada)   123

Behind the scenes

Here are some excerpts from a book written by an American journalist who accompanied the Beatles on many of their tours:

Before the performance begins, a girl in the front row, with 'Beatles' written in gold on her red jacket, has to be forcibly held down by her friend in the next seat.

Backstage, Paul is playing the piano with a sweater over his head. Ringo and George are putting on make-up, and John is ostentatiously removing the glasses he constantly wears off-stage. 'Mustn't spoil the image,' he says. They come on to the platform, and the screaming begins.

Paul announces the numbers and the girls sit with their hands clenching their faces as if they have just seen a vision. John makes threatening gestures to the audience with his fist. It brings more screams. 'In sweet fragrant meadows,' sings Paul, nodding his head angelically. 'With a love like that,' sing Paul and George, and a blonde woman starts to rush the stage. The policewomen in the aisles move in and lead her away. 'Twist and shout,' bawls John. 'C'mon, work it all out.' The sound is deafening. Hordes of jelly-babies are thrown on stage. Several autograph books, a doll, a shoe, and an umbrella wind up there also.

As they finish, a girl in a red sweater is reaching for the stage, shouting 'John, John'. 'The Queen' starts. She is comforted by her friend. As the anthem ends she walks out limply.

. . . Neil Aspinall *(their road manager)* sits in a corner signing pictures of the Beatles. He has perfected their signatures, and these are being kept in anticipation of future requests.

. . . Epstein *(their manager)* persuaded Capitol, the Beatles' American recording company, to spend fifty thousand dollars for what they called a 'crash publicity program'.

They plastered five million 'The Beatles Are Coming' stickers on telephone poles, washroom walls, and other appropriate places throughout the country. They distributed the record the Beatles had made in London to every disc jockey in the country. They issued a four-page newspaper on the Beatles and sent out a million copies. They photographed their top executives wearing Beatle wigs and distributed 'Be a Beatle Booster' badges to all their employees. They offered Beatle haircuts free to all their female employees and persuaded Janet Leigh to get one. They even tried, unsuccessfully, to bribe a University of Washington cheer-leader into holding up a card reading 'The Beatles Are Coming' to the television cameras at the Rose Bowl.

. . . To prepare for their trip to the States . . . they *(The Beatles)* went to the EMI studios to record an 'open-end interview'. This was a prolonged introduction to their record which would be sent to American disc jockeys. By means of a prepared form the disc jockey would ask questions that fitted the answers the Beatles were recording in London and thus gave the impression he was interviewing them himself.

. . . Paul explained that they never talk to the teenage magazines. 'They just make it up. I think they prefer it that way.'

From *Love Me Do* by Michael Braun

A musician's view

Let us look at the content of an average Top Twenty hit and see why it is cast in the particular mould which we all know so well.

A good deal has been written about the lyrics of pop songs. Partly this is because it is always easier to write about words than about music; nevertheless, the lines to which the top tunes are set are in themselves revealing.

Obviously the theme must be relevant—that is to say, it must be 'about' one of the universal themes which appeal to all. Of these, the boy-girl motif is the surest winner, more especially since the growth of the teen-age market has led to a special assault on that section of the community.

. . . But, as has frequently been pointed out, it must be love of a very romantic and sentimental nature . . . There may occasionally be the lyric of the frustrated lover, but it is never the frustration of everyday human circumstance; always the singer and the object of his or her song inhabit a dream world, seated as it were on remote clouds of insubstantial candy-floss, with nothing to think about but their romantic emotions.

In this respect there is a great difference between the real folk jazz and the pop. The blues singer did not tell of an idealised world but of a very real one where pain and trouble were common experiences—where music and song might help you to overcome trouble but not by pretending it didn't exist.

. . . Just as the words take a basic, universal theme, denude it of any real individuality of utterance, and serve it up for mass commercial consumption, so the music is standardised to a pattern. It is stated that an electronic brain has been invented which can 'compose' melodies; and there would seem no logical reason why in fact a robot machine could not produce at least a passable imitation of a pop tune.

. . . If a record is to sell as near as maybe a million copies, the tune must be something which appeals instantly to as many as possible. Now, with the greatest melodies of the world, whether classical or folk, one can often say that when you have heard them you feel that they could not have been otherwise, that each note as it is played or sung seems to follow inevitably from the one before; yet the greatness of the tune and its composer lies precisely in the fact that none of us could ourselves have imagined that melody if we had never heard it before, not even if we had been given the first phrase. But a melody tune for the Top Twenty must take at once, and to do this it is necessary that from the start it shall follow the expected path. Given the opening phrase, any average composer could finish the tune and the result would be very much what is eventually published.

. . . We come now to the performer, the recording artist.

In folk music proper the performer is important because of his direct creative contribution. An enthusiast looks on the label of a jazz record not for the composer of a piece, but for the performers. In pops the performer's personality is important, but for a rather different reason. For the number to take, the record-buyer must be able to identify himself with it; just as the theme must be one of the universals, so the singer should be an ordinary chap—one of us. The teen-age idol need bring no very great musical or technical skill to his work; but he must attract the fans, and they must be able to feel that the romantic idealised world in which he lives (in public) is one which they, Walter Mitty-like, may too inhabit.

From an article by Donald Hughes in
Discrimination and Popular Culture

Teen-age tyranny

It is through the mass media that the images and desires of teen-agers are at once standardised and distorted. The printed word, the television screen, the movies and that no man's land between art and entertainment—the record industry—simultaneously extract the flashiest, most obscene and less meaningful aspects of adolescence and crystallise this titillating mixture into a commercial formula which is then beamed at teen-age America.

Violence and frenzy—substitutes for real action and motion—are always present either as the main theme or leitmotif. The family, if it is not actually in a state of total disintegration, is never free from open or thinly camouflaged hostility . . . In literature, the adventurous Tom Sawyer has been replaced by the lost and unloved Holden Caulfield of *Catcher in the Rye*. Instead of drifting down a lazy river, teen-agers of modern literature drag-race down an aimless road of meaningless danger or get themselves senselessly beaten by a pimp in a flea-bag hotel.

Many of today's plots stress victory without effort, except for brief flashes of violence. Instead of the worship of heroes

·who have triumphed after long labors and privations, the modern teen-age idols win with a punch in the nose.

. . . Hero worship is an important part of adolescence. Youngsters grow up with models of manhood or womanhood in their minds. Their goals, aspirations and behavior are constantly influenced by these models.

What are today's teen-age heroes really like?

The most important common denominator of most teen-age idols is that they are mass-produced. They are not really people, with individual characteristics and personalities: they appear to have been made in a mold. They are managed. They are 'handled' commercially. They did not grow; they were manufactured by press agents, publicity departments and the vast and efficient machinery of public relations. Their success story is told almost entirely by dollar signs, Cadillacs and swimming pools. They share with teen-agers a semiliterate jargon and an almost total absence of original ideas. Yet, in an obscenely labored way, they strive to be 'wholesome'. They love 'Mom and Dad' and moon over childhood sweethearts turned child brides.

. . . Teen-agers seem to identify their heroes mainly by the songs with which each is linked. But to the uninitiated, most of these singers appear to be the product of an assembly line, as interchangeable as the packages of detergents in the supermarket. They not only sound alike, they look alike as well, partly because of the standardisation of their mannerisms.

. . . It is not at all startling to show-biz experts that many of these 'singers' cannot sing in public because they have been literally put together by and on tape. Their records consist of elaborate splicings of tape to eliminate mistakes. Lack of natural volume in their voices is overcome by the 'echo chamber', which gives their recorded songs not only a petulantly wailing and barely comprehensible quality but makes them sound as though they were singing in a fish tank.

In many instances lack of real talent is so complete an obstacle to any personal performance in public that the young 'artist' just mouths the words and hopes that the public-address system which carries his pre-recorded voice will not break down. This novel form of 'singing' in public is known in the trade as 'lip sync.' It is the serious counterpart of one of the oldest vaudeville comedy acts—and it is not intended to be funny. Its purpose is to eliminate talent as a prerequisite for the performing arts.

While not all teen-age singers use this extreme technique for 'legitimate' deception, most of them rely on accompanying tricks and gestures to put their songs over and make the audience judge and love them for reasons other than their mournfully synthetic voices. Never has the public been given such a variety of swaying, hip-swinging and, of course, the inevitable finger-snapping. These mannerisms are frequently the only 'comprehensible' part of a performance which puts a premium on unintelligible diction.

Because the heroes worshipped by adolescents inevitably color their young admirers' ideas and ideals, they cannot help but influence the teen-agers' concept of the qualities needed to rise to fame and fortune.

The only thing these modern heroes have in common with the old Horatio Alger (*an American author who wrote stories about the rise of poor boys from rags to riches*) legends, however, is that most of them did start as poor boys who wanted to make good. Few, if any, of them thought of themselves as singers or had any strong urge to excel as artists. Popular singing simply seemed the quickest and easiest road to the financial top. And the road is lined with instant glamour.

Almost invariably, the search for success starts with the preliminary search for a manager. Behind almost every teenage millionaire is that modern Miracle Man—the agent. Usually, an older man, wise in the ways of press-agentry, manipulation of fan clubs, the do's and don't's of discjockeying for position, contacts with celebrities and gossip columnists and expertise with booking agents, is to be credited with the creation of the manufactured idols.

. . . Today's adults, in their thirties and forties, may look back at the beginning of Frank Sinatra's career, with its headlines about swooning bobby-soxers, and ask: 'What's so different now?'

Sinatra was, of course, among the first of the singers to

be discovered by teen-agers and to grow up to be an adult performer. But there is a difference. First of all, Sinatra could sing. He had real talent that was not created by mechanical devices. His career today, though by no means harmed by publicity and press-agentry, is based on proven ability as a crooner and, since his role in *From Here to Eternity,* as an actor as well.

. . . American civilisation tends to stand in such awe of its teen-age segment that it is in danger of becoming a teen-age society, with permanently teen-age standards of thought, culture and goals. As a result, American society is growing down rather than growing up.

This is a creeping disease, not unlike hardening of the arteries. It is a softening of adulthood. It leads to immature goals in music, art and literature. It forces newspapers, television producers and movie-makers to translate the adult English usage into the limited vocabulary of the teen-culture. It opens up vast opportunities for commercial exploitation and thereby sets off a chain reaction which constantly strengthens teen-age tyranny.

It is a tyranny that dominates most brutally the teen-agers themselves. What starts with relatively innocent conforming to the ways of the crowd soon turns into manipulation of those crowd *mores (standards of behaviour)* by a combination of inept adult leadership and plain commercial exploitation. The longer it continues, the harder it becomes, as in the case of every artificially imposed regime, for dissenters to declare their independence.

We are fully aware that not all teen-agers and their parents have fallen victim to teen-age tyranny. Many have retained their freedom and upheld their standards. But even those who have resisted the trend know that the stronger the tide the harder it becomes to move against it.

From *Teen-age Tyranny* by Grace and Fred M. Hechtinger

9 Vivisection

Each year in Great Britain over four million experiments are carried out on living animals. Here is a description of one of them taken from 'The Lancet'.

Unanaesthetised dogs and goats were exposed to phosgene *(a lung-irritant gas used in chemical warfare)* in a static chamber and were transfused sixteen hours after exposure . . . Two dogs were exposed to phosgene concentration for 10 minutes. Both were very ill 16 hours later, with laboured respiration, cyanosis, and collapsed peripheral veins . . . After transfusion the symptoms became worse, one dog dying two hours after transfusion, and the other seven hours after transfusion.

A publicity photograph supplied by the Scottish Society for the **Prevention of Vivisection.**

Animals or Humans?

Until 1921 there was no effective treatment for diabetes. In that year, two young Canadian scientists, Frederick Banting and Charles Best, began experiments on dogs in an effort to obtain a substance called Insulin. They believed that it was the lack of this substance, manufactured in the pancreas, that caused diabetes in humans. So they tied up the ducts of the pancreas of living dogs, hoping that six weeks later, after the pancreas had degenerated, they would be able to obtain Insulin from it. Their first experiments were unsuccessful but eventually they were able to extract some Insulin. They then tested its effect by injecting it into dogs which had been made diabetic by the surgical removal of the pancreas.

The date was July 30th. Although the first few injections were not dramatic in their effect, it soon became evident that they had, indeed, found a method for producing a substance which would lower the blood sugar and the sugar in the urine *(symptoms of diabetes)*. Excited by this first success, they pressed on, and during the weeks from August 14th, they worked night and day on a succession of diabetic dogs, using extract after extract to produce the dramatic life-saving result.

. . . The excitement of those days can still be recalled very vividly by those who took part in all these experimental activities. Banting and Best repeated their experiments over and over again, proving beyond a shadow of doubt that they had discovered an internal secretion of the pancreas; that a method had been developed which enabled them to prepare a potent anti-diabetic extract which would keep a diabetic dog alive for many weeks.

The next hurdle to be crossed was the preparation of material that could be used for the treatment of human beings. As the news spread, desperate people began to ask how lives might be saved, and soon the pressure for application to human beings became very great.

. . . A young boy named Leonard Thompson in January 1922 was the first patient to experience the miraculous effects of Insulin. Leonard's diabetes was discovered in 1920, when he was only 11 years old. In spite of the starvation diet on which he was placed, he went steadily down hill, and when admitted to hospital weighed only 65 pounds. He was on a diet of only 450 calories, or about as much food as an ordinary boy of that age would eat in one meal. Already the dread smell of acetone (the same substance that is in some nail polish removers) could be smelled on his breath. In his urine there was further evidence of this substance circulating in the blood stream. His abdomen was enlarged, the muscles were wasted, and his hair had begun to come out. He showed the appalling weakness of the diabetic nearing death, and already he had to spend most of his time in bed.

This was the ideal case on which to attempt treatment with Insulin. Banting and Best knew about such patients from their friends at the Toronto General Hospital nearby. Between Christmas and New Year they had some time available to prepare an extract of Insulin like those they had been using on diabetic dogs with such success. They debated whether they should use adult beef pancreas to prepare the extract or, alternatively, that from unborn calves, material they already knew to be so much more potent and freer of impurities. In the end, it was decided that they would use the adult beef pancreas because they believed that their extract would save a human diabetic's life, and that there would follow immediately a tremendous demand for this material. They argued that it would not be very easy to secure enough foetal material to go round, and that the first demonstration should be with pancreas from adult animals which was abundantly available. They, therefore, set about the preparation of the Insulin. Best used precisely the same technique that he had been using for the past fifteen weeks, and when the fluid was ready he and Banting each gave the other a dose of this material under the skin of their upper arms. A little redness and swelling appeared, but since neither of them was diabetic it was not possible to demonstrate the other effects, which they knew, from their animal experiments, that it possessed.

Now they were ready for the great test on human beings,

and they took the extract to the Toronto General Hospital where it was to be used by Dr. Walter Campbell. The parents of this patient-to-be have told of their terrible distress after their local doctor in the east end of Toronto had discovered that their boy, Leonard, had *diabetes mellitus*. In the most moving terms, Leonard's father describes the scene when the boy's doctor offered him the opportunity to have Insulin treatment. He said to the doctors, 'I do not know what this substance is. This boy is old enough now to decide for himself, and you must tell him precisely what the chances are and what the risks of the treatment are.' In one of the small, dimly-lit rooms, the house doctor and physician carefully explained to the boy that a new kind of fluid, made in one of the departments of the University, had become available. When the boy was asked if he would like to have this treatment, he looked at his father, who nodded encouragingly, and said, 'Yes, I would like to have it.' This particular extract, although it was potent and reduced the sugar in the blood and urine of the young patient to normal limits, also produced a reddening and swelling in the skin of the arm. Perhaps it was due to the boy's lowered resistance or to other unknown factors, but whatever the cause, he did develop a swelling and redness and the injections had to be discontinued. In a few days, more supplies of Insulin had been produced, and since the effect of the treatment on the general condition had been so dramatic, the injections were resumed. From that day on he began to make a steady recovery. He remained well on his diet, gained weight and resumed a normal life. He might well be alive today had he not been badly injured in a motor-cycle accident several years later. He died of pneumonia, a very difficult disease to treat in those days before adequate therapy had been developed.

Now, with the first dramatic demonstration that Insulin would produce its effect on human beings, as well as on diabetic dogs, the tempo quickened. Other patients at the Toronto General Hospital were given Insulin, and they, too, demonstrated the same fall in sugar in the blood and disappearance of sugar from the urine. Wasted, emaciated individuals began to recover. Dr. A. A. Fletcher and

Dr. W. R. Campbell began an intensive study of the clinical use of Insulin. At another hospital in the city, where veterans were treated, Banting worked with his old friend, Dr. Joseph Gilchrist, himself a diabetic, and set up further clinical trials. Soon the whole world was knocking on the door for information about the new Insulin and how to treat diabetic patients with it.

. . . There are said to be more than fifteen million diabetics alive in the world today; for each of them, and for their families, the wonder never ceases, and their gratitude to Banting and Best cannot be measured.

From *The Story of Insulin* by Professor
G. A. Wrenshall, Dr. G. Hetenyi and
Dr. W. R. Feasby

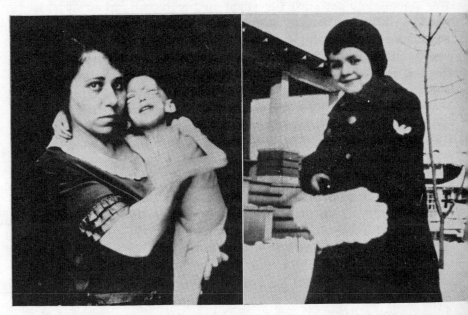

One of the first patients to be treated with insulin. Left: before injections began. Right: 32 days later.

VIVISECTION

By CHARLES RICHARD CAMMELL

PERHAPS the most disgusting and sordid part of all the vile business of Vivisection is the public attitude towards it. What is the public answer to our denunciations of the monstrous crimes of our laboratories ? It is always this : " You cannot stop Vivisection because it is the means by which so many cures are found for human illness."

I am sick and tired of telling people that Vivisection is of no use to them, and of *proving* to them that it is of no use to them ; that Claude Bernard himself, the High Priest of Experimental Science, died with the cry of despair on his lips, " Nos mains sont toujours vides ! " ; that the hands of the Vivisector will always be empty ; that the noise of his vaunted discoveries dies down, and that nothing solid, nothing real, remains to him — nothing but the massed agony of millions of terrified and tortured creatures, mad with pain and fear. By such means as the Vivisectors no good thing *can* ever come to Humanity. By a mysterious and fundamental law, at once physical and metaphysical — a most Divine law — Good cannot be born of Evil. *God is just. His mercy is but for the merciful.* No nation that tolerates the practice of Vivisection deserves that any good should come to it ; nor will any good come to it. Peace will not remain with it ; it does not deserve Peace ; it deserves War, and it will get War, with all its scientific horrors, which are prepared in those very laboratories where the faithful dumb friends of man are so ruthlessly repaid by him for their fidelity.

Yes, I am weary of showing people how useless a thing Vivisection is to them. I do not care a straw if it is of use to them or not. A man or a woman who is such a craven and such a wretch as to wish to save his life — to remain at best for a few more short years in this world of care — by permitting and encouraging the unspeakable abominations of Vivisection, is better dead. We do not want a world full of sickly brutes and cowards who have been kept alive by crimes. We want a world of decent people, who look life *and* death in the face, and who would scorn " to save themselves a twinge of pain " (as Robert Browning put it) by causing incalculable suffering to defenceless creatures. What sort of people is the world made up of, if this is the one reason why Vivisection is tolerated ; that it serves to keep cravens alive, when Nature would have them dead ?

In the Holy Crusade against Vivisection not so much would I put before people the utter uselessness of that monstrous practice ; rather would I put them to shame by reason of their contemptible and cruel cowardice in for one moment entertaining the idea of wishing to save their own mortal bodies by countenancing such immoralities as those committed in the name of Experimental Science. I am loth to believe that the world is utterly shameless. I hesitate to believe that the majority of people in this or any other country, are as callous of cruelty, or as cowardly as they appear to be from the attitude they adopt towards Vivisection. Rather would I deem that they are still ignorant of the depth of its horrors ; rather would I believe that if they once really knew of what is going on under the false pretence of the public welfare, they would repudiate it — would *denounce* and *renounce* Vivisection for ever. We must arouse their sense of shame. We want a world of decent people, not a world of cravens who look to the sadist in the Laboratory to keep their bodies alive by any means, however execrable, when the time has come for their souls to move onward.

Reprinted by

The Scottish Society for the Prevention of Vivisection

President :
Miss LIND-AF-HAGEBY

Chairman :
A. C. T. NISBET, Esq.

OFFICE—10 QUEENSFERRY STREET EDINBURGH 2

Life Membership £5
Ordinary Membership 5s. Associates 2/6

138

One doctor's opinion

Consider the type of person performing experiments on animals—all medical men or scientists engaged in medical research. These men are working for the good of mankind, and mankind owes a great debt of gratitude to them for this fundamental research.

No man wittingly brings about the failure of his own work. Research must be accurate to be of value, and the worker must ensure consistent working conditions and exclude complications. Only well-managed, healthy stock can provide the necessary material suitable for the work medical research demands. Inferior, disease-ridden animals do not accurately imitate conditions found in man, and lead to erroneous results.

No man, having spent long years of training in the great humanitarian traditions of medicine and veterinary surgery, would be so stupid as to ruin his own work by using unsuitable material.

The Medical Research Council Laboratory keeps details of supply, management, and breeding of laboratory animals, and provides a list of accredited animal dealers.

Clearly, it is useless to use stolen animals of uncertain origin, or animals abandoned by owners and left to pick up disease in the streets. These animals are often destroyed by the R.S.P.C.A. if not claimed; as laboratory animals they would be far better cared for than many a homeless, mangy beast.

Medical research today is greatly dependent on vivisection. Infant mortalities through smallpox, polio, tetanus, diphtheria, whooping cough and tuberculosis bear no comparison today with those occurring years ago, almost entirely because of research on animals.

Take polio as an example: three monkeys are needed to provide enough vaccine to immunise 1,000 children, and some 2,500 children must be immunised to prevent one case of polio. The question we must all ask ourselves is this, which would we rather have, a child crippled—perhaps for life—by paralytic poliomyelitis, or eight monkeys flown from India, treated at all times humanely then painlessly killed?

To the small amount of surgical work performed on animals—under anaesthetics and with fully aseptic techniques—we owe some of the more spectacular advances in human surgery. 'Hole in the heart' operations, skin grafting after burns, corneal grafts, kidney transplanting, abdominal and thoracic surgery, brain surgery, and a marked reduction in the incidence of cancer in certain industrial trades—all these advances can be directly attributed to research with animals.

We are all concerned with the need to find a cure for cancer of all kinds. But first the causes must be determined—work which is greatly dependent on animal experiment.

I am always ironically amused by a lady in my district who, on even Saturdays, exhorts me to give for cancer research and on odd Saturdays tells me at great length how wicked she thinks vivisection is. This well-meaning but foolish soul is being sadly deceived.

An article in *She*

The Littlewood Report

In 1965 the Departmental Committee on Experiments on Animals (Chairman: Sir Sydney Littlewood) recommended that greater protection should be afforded to laboratory animals, that the Inspectorate should be increased from six to 21, that experiments should be restricted to animals bred for that purpose, and that the facts of animal experimentation (they thought this a better name than vivisection) should be made more accessible to the public. Here are some excerpts from their Report:

The written evidence submitted by the National Anti-Vivisection Society consisted for the most part of extracts from a number of reports of experiments (in foreign countries as well as in the United Kingdom) published in scientific journals. The Society told us that 'this batch of evidence' was mainly concerned with one form of experiment, i.e. the introduction of electrodes, chemicals, etc., into the cranial cavity of cats; that it showed that many of the experiments were 'repetitive', gave different results under different hands and in different places, and were liable to be misleading; and that it was evident the animals had been caused 'extreme distress and suffering'. The Society said that they had evidence of other lines of research which had been pursued in such a manner as to cause 'severe suffering' e.g. in drug-testing on the eyes of living animals, induction of shock by infliction of severe injuries (crushing and battering limbs), exsanguination, impeding circulation of blood. We were not, however, provided with this evidence. We examined with care the illustrative material submitted and paid particular attention to the experiments reported to have been carried out on cats at the National Institute for Medical Research. In the course of our visit to this institution we saw several cats with cannulae surgically inserted in the cranial cavity for subsequent administration of drugs, and noted their appearance of complete well-being and friendliness. We also saw a film made of the surgical preparation and a subsequent film record of a cat's reaction to a drug administered via the cranial cavity. We met the licensee concerned and satisfied ourselves both that the experimental techniques employed were humane and that the experiments cited by the Society —part of a long series designed to elucidate the mechanism of epilepsy and of the action of drugs on the central nervous system—were justifiable under the terms of the Act *(Cruelty to Animals Act,* 1876).

. . . The British Pharmacopoeia Commission said that in successive editions of the British Pharmacopoeia a number of biological tests had been replaced by newly accepted chemical tests. For example, biological assay of tubocurarine chloride by rats or rabbits and a test using the rat for abnormal toxicity in dimercaprol were replaced by chemical procedures in 1958. The Commission emphasised its view that 'biological tests are usually much more costly than chemical or physical methods in materials, overheads, expert staff and time.' . . . We were not able to discover any instance where there had been undue delay in dispensing with a prescribed test, and are satisfied that all concerned in the formulation of prescribed tests are anxious not to waste animals by retaining biological tests longer than necessary.

. . . According to the Home Office none of the police forces regarded the stealing of cats and dogs as a problem and none of them had any evidence to suggest that stolen animals are being sold to medical research laboratories.

In order to understand the table of statistics reproduced opposite, it is necessary to know the significance of the different types of certificate mentioned.

Certificate A was required for any experiment carried out without an anaesthetic. It was granted only when the use of an anaesthetic would have frustrated the purpose of the experiment. In practice it was granted only when no operation was involved or when it was one that involved no appreciable pain (e.g. inoculation).

Certificate B was required when an animal that was going to die as the result of the experiment was to be allowed to regain consciousness first. It was granted only when killing it before it regained consciousness would have frustrated the object of the experiment.

Certificate C was required when an experiment was to be carried out for demonstration purposes in medical schools, hospitals, etc.

Certificate E or EE was required before an operation without an anaesthetic could be carried out on a dog or a cat. Dogs and cats could only be used if they were essential for the success of the experiment.

Certificate F was required if an experiment was to be carried out on a horse, ass or mule. It was only granted if the use of these animals was essential for the success of the experiment. In practice such experiments were almost entirely confined to veterinary practice and the investigation of the diseases of horses.

The Littlewood Committee recommended that this complicated system of certificates should be replaced by the issue of a single licence that specified the types of experiments allowed.

The Littlewood Committee had been asked 'to consider the present control over experiments on living animals, and to consider whether, and if so what, changes are desirable in the law or its administration'. However they thought it right to draw attention to three major questions which lay outside their terms of reference. These were:

1 Who can say whether, if certain biological tests were forbidden, satisfactory chemical or other methods of testing would not be developed?

2 Who is responsible for establishing whether modern medical techniques, with their emphasis on immunology and

STATISTICS

	1885	1910	1920	1930	1939	1950	1960	1963
Number of licensees	53	542	776	1,459	2,249	3,780	6,872	8,789
Number of licensees who performed no experiments ...	9	147	275	362	645	1,006	1,989	2,857
Number of active licensees	44	395	501	1,097	1,604	2,774	4,983	5,932
Total experiments	797	95,731	70,367	450,822	954,691	1,779,215	3,701,184	4,196,566
Experiments under licence alone								
Certificate A	210	2,718	2,027	7,555	9,653	27,266	47,225	70,256
Certificate B	382	90,792	63,374	432,519	907,481	1,538,308	3,345,464	3,786,448
Certificate C	123	1,997	4,718	10,051	36,737	211,428	304,160	323,334
	82	224	248	697	820	2,213	4,335	4,227
Number of experiments in which cats, dogs or equidae were used:								
(i) Certificates A, B, E, EE, F	9	1,161	480	3,383	5,301	4,421	8,554	12,291
(ii) Under anaesthesia throughout ...	N.A.	N.A.	N.A.	N.A.	N.A.	5,238	9,593	12,144
Number of experiments in cancer research	N.A.	49,662	6,136	25,259	26,936	78,192	229,751	269,658
Number of experiments for diagnosis	N.A.	N.A.	10,505	49,741	N.A.	202,358	218,931	318,851
Number of experiments performed for standardisation and testing of sera, vaccine or drugs	N.A.	8,000	27,000	181,000	296,813	596,813	1,236,585	1,173,535
Number of registered places	13	69	204	285	433	478	524	556
Number of Inspectors (in post)	1	2	3	2	3	4	5	6
Number of visits by Inspectors	N.A.	N.A.	N.A.	N.A.	829	1,232	1,506	1,941

drug therapy, both of which are inseparable from animal experimentation, are developing medical practice in the right direction?

3 Who is to take responsibility for moral or ethical judgment in the use of animals for experimental purposes as such?

"*All things bright and beautiful,*
All creatures great and small,
All things wise and wonderful,
The Lord God made them all."

Sprod.

Is vivisection any worse than this?

10 A matter of life or death

Pearl Buck, the famous novelist, is the mother of a mentally handicapped child. She describes what this has meant to her.

How often did I cry out in my heart that it would be better if my child died! If that shocks you who do not know, it will not shock those who do know. I would have welcomed death for my child and would still welcome it, for then she would be finally safe.

It is inevitable that one ponders much on this matter of a kindly death. Every now and again I see in the newspapers the report of a man or woman who has put to death a mentally defective child. My heart goes out to such a one. I understand the love and despair which prompted the act. There is not only the despair that descends when the inevitable makes itself known, but there is the increasing despair of every day. For each day that makes clear that the child is only as he was yesterday drives the despair deeper, and there are besides the difficulties of care for such a child, the endless round of duties that seem to bear no fruit, tending a body that will be no more than a body however long it lives, gazing into the dull eyes that respond with no lively look, helping the fumbling hands—all these drive deeper the despair. And added to the despair is the terror and the question, 'Who will do this in case I do not live?'

And yet I know that the parents of whom I read do wrong when they take to themselves a right which is not theirs and end the physical lives of their children. In love they may do it, and yet it is wrong. There is a sacred quality of life which none of us can fathom. All peoples feel it, for in all societies it is considered a sin for one human being to kill another for a reason of his own. Society decrees death for certain crimes, but the innocent may not be killed, and there is none more innocent than these children who never grow up. Murder remains murder. Were the right to kill a child put even into a parent's hands, the effect would be evil indeed in our world. Were the right to kill any innocent person assumed by society, the effect would be monstrous. For first it might be only the helpless children who were killed, but then it might seem right to kill the helpless old; and then the conscience would become so dulled that prejudice would give the right to kill, and persons of a certain colour or creed might be destroyed. The only safety is to reject completely the possibility of death as a means of ending any innocent life, however useless. The damage is not to the one who is killed, but to the one who kills. Euthanasia is a long, smooth-sounding word, and it conceals its danger as long, smooth words do, but the danger is there, nevertheless.

It would be evasion, however, if I pretended that it was easy to accept the inevitable. For the sake of others who are walking that stony road, I will say that my inner rebellion lasted for many years. My common sense, my convictions of duty, all told me that I must not let the disaster spoil my own life or those of relatives and friends. But common sense and duty cannot always prevail when the heart is broken. My compromise was to learn how to act on the surface as much like my usual self as possible, to talk, to laugh, to seem to take an interest in what went on. Underneath the rebellion burned, and tears flowed the moment I was alone.

. . . The children who never grow are human beings and they suffer as human beings, inarticulately but deeply nevertheless. The human creature is always more than an animal. That is the one thing we must never forget. He is forever more than a beast. Though the mind has gone away, though he cannot speak or communicate with anyone, the human stuff is there, and he belongs to the human family.

I saw this wonderfully exemplified in one state institution. When I first visited the place it was an abode of horror. The children, some young in body, some old, were apparently without any minds whatever. The average mental age was estimated at less than one year. They were herded together like dogs. They wore bag-like garments of rough calico or burlap. Their food was given to them on the floor and they snatched it up. No effort was made to teach them toilet habits. The floors were of cement and were hosed two or three times a day. The beds were pallets on the floor, and filthy. There were explanations, of course. I was told that these children could be taught nothing, that they merely existed until they died. Worst of all to me was that there was not one thing of beauty anywhere, nothing for the children to look at, no reason for them to lift their heads or put out their hands.

Some years later I went back again. I had heard there was a new man in charge, a young man who was different. I found that he was different, and because he was, he had made the whole institution different. It was as crowded as ever, but wholly changed. It was like a home. There were gay curtains at the windows and bright linoleums on the floors. In the various rooms the children had been segregated, babies were with babies, and older children with their own kind. There were chairs and benches and the children sat on them. There were flowers in the windows and toys on the floor. The children were decent and even wore pretty clothes, and they were all clean. The old sickening smell was gone. There was a dining-room, and there were tables, on which were dishes and spoons and mugs.

'Are the children now of a higher grade?' I asked the young man.

'No,' he said, smiling, 'many of them are the same children.'

'But I was told they could not be taught.'

'They can all be taught something,' he replied. 'When they can't manage alone, someone helps them.'

Then he showed me the things they had made, actually little baskets and mats, simple and full of mistakes, but to me wonderful. And the children who had made them were so proud of what they had done. They came up to us, and though they could not speak, they knew what they had done.

'Has their mental age gone up?' I asked.

'A little, on the average,' he replied. 'But it isn't only mental age that counts with them—or with anybody, for that matter.'

'How did you do it?' I asked.

'I treat them as human beings,' he said simply.

. . . My helpless child has taught me so much. She has taught me patience, above all else. I come of a family impatient with stupidity and slowness, and I absorbed the family intolerance of minds less quick than our own. Then there was put into my sole keeping this pitiful mind, struggling against I know not what handicap. Could I despise it for what was no fault of its own? That indeed would have been the most cruel injustice. While I tried to find out its slight abilities I was compelled both by love and justice to learn tender and careful patience. It was not always easy. Natural impatience burst forth time and again, to my shame, and it seemed useless to try to teach. But justice reasoned with me thus: 'This mind has the right to its fullest development too. It may be very little, but the right is the same as yours, or any other's. If you refuse it the right to know, in so far as it can know, you do a wrong.'

So by this most sorrowful way I was compelled to tread, I learned respect and reverence for every human mind. It was my child who taught me to understand so clearly that all people are equal in their humanity and that all have the same human rights. None is to be considered less, as a human being, than any other, and each must be given his place and his safety in the world. I might never have learned this in any other way. I might have gone on in the arrogance of my own intolerance for those less able than myself. My child taught me humility.

. . . The minds of retarded children are sane minds, normal except that, being arrested, the processes are slowed. But they learn in the same ways that the normal minds do, repeated many more times. Psychologists, observing the slower processes, have been able to discover, exactly as though in a slow-motion picture, the way the human creature acquires new knowledge and new habits. Our educational techniques for normal children have been vastly improved by what the retarded children have taught us.

. . . No child ought to be merely something to be cared for and preserved from harm. His life, however simple, means something. He has something to contribute, even though he is helpless. There are reasons for his condition, causes which may be discovered. If he himself cannot be cured or even changed, others may be born whole because of what he has been able to teach, all unknowingly.

The Training School at Vineland is an excellent example of what I mean. For many years it has maintained an active research department . . . Its work with birth-injured children and cerebral palsy has been notable, and the vigorous men and women who have spent their lives there learning from the children, in order that they may know better how to prevent and to cure, have infused vitality into the life of the institution, and into the whole subject of mental deficiency beyond.

Parents may find comfort, I say, in knowing that their children are not useless, but that their lives, limited as they are, are of great potential value to the human race. We learn as much from sorrow as from joy, as much from illness as from health, from handicap as from advantage—and indeed perhaps more. Not out of fullness has the human soul always reached its highest, but often out of deprivation. This is not to say that sorrow is better than happiness, illness than health, poverty than riches. Had I been given the choice, I would a thousand times over have chosen to have my child sound and whole, a normal woman today, living a woman's life. I miss eternally the person she cannot be. I am not resigned and never will be. Resignation is something still and dead, an inactive acceptance that bears no fruit. On the contrary, I rebel against the unknown fate that fell upon her somewhere and stopped her growth. Such things ought not to be, and because it has happened to me and because I know what this sorrow is I devote myself and my child to the work of doing all we can to prevent such suffering for others.

. . . So what I would say to parents is something I have learned through the years and it took me long to learn it, and I am still learning. When your little child is born to you not whole and sound as you had hoped, but warped and defective in body or mind or perhaps both, remember this is still your child. Remember, too, that the child has his right to life, whatever that life may be, and he has the right to happiness, which you must find for him. Be proud of your child, accept him as he is and do not heed the words and stares of those who know no better. This child has a meaning for you and for all children. You will find a joy you cannot now suspect in fulfilling his life for and with him. Lift up your head and go your appointed way.

I speak as one who knows.

From *The Child Who Never Grew* by Pearl S. Buck

The Right to Life

The Nazi policy of compulsory euthanasia was introduced by a secret order of Hitler of September 1, 1939. At first it was confined to the Germans but it was subsequently extended to foreigners. Altogether 275,000 people died in the German euthanasia centres. A great many of these were foreign slave labourers who were meant to be suffering from incurable tuberculosis. After the war some of those responsible were brought to justice. Euthanasia of foreign citizens was held to be a crime against international law. The trial of the officials of the Hadamar Sanatorium proceeded on the technical basis that no state has the right to deprive a foreigner of his life except after conviction of a crime carrying the death penalty before a properly constituted tribunal.

What of voluntary euthanasia? Compulsory taking of another person's life is one thing: taking it with his consent is another. Of course anyone tired of life is able to kill himself and nothing the law or anyone else can do is able to stop him, once such an intention has been finally formed. Euthanasia does not normally concern such people. It covers the incurably sick, perhaps in great pain, who have little or no hope of recovery and whose death appears to be only a matter of time. Do they have the right to consent to their own extinction? And may doctors, nurses, or relatives assist them to bring such an end about?

English law does not countenance any form of euthanasia. Doctors or others who either assist sick persons to kill themselves or actually kill them themselves are guilty of criminal offences. Aiding or abetting another person to kill himself carries a penalty of imprisonment for a term not exceeding fourteen years. If doctors or others do the killing themselves they are principals in the first degree to murder, even if the patient has given his consent. In practice under such circumstances a doctor would be more likely to be held guilty of manslaughter. As Mr. Justice Byles said as long ago as 1862 in the case of *Regina v Murton*: 'If a man is suffering from a disease which in all likelihood would terminate his life in a short time, and another gives him a wound or hurt which hastens his death, this is such a killing as constitutes murder or at least manslaughter.'

The administration of the law is more lenient in practice than its theory indicates. Before the Homicide Act of 1957, which set up new categories of capital and non-capital murder, it was normal to reprieve those who had been convicted of murder and therefore been sentenced to death, by reason of a mercy killing. Indeed the Royal Commission on Capital Punishment referred to reprieve as 'a foregone conclusion'. In 1934, for example, Mrs. Brownhill was tried for murder. She had had a serious operation and was worried about the future of her thirty-one-year-old imbecile son if she did not survive. She killed the son by gassing and administering aspirin. The death sentence was passed but the jury had entered a strong recommendation for mercy and two days later she was reprieved. After three months in prison she was pardoned. The irony of the case is that the operation was completely successful. Another case with a similar result was that of Mr. Long in 1946 who gassed his imbecile seven-year-old daughter and was sentenced to death. A week later he was reprieved and the death sentence commuted to one of life imprisonment, the time of his release being within the discretion of the Home Secretary.

. . . In the pre-Christian era various forms of euthanasia were practised. In primitive societies abandonment of the aged is a common feature but it was not practised in Greece or Rome. (In India at one time it was customary to take the old to the banks of the Ganges, fill their mouths and noses with sacred mud and throw them into the river.) Child exposure was, however, known in Greece. 'The question arises,' writes Aristotle in his *Politics,* 'whether children should always be reared or may sometimes be exposed to die. There should certainly be a law to prevent the rearing of deformed children. On the other hand there should also be a law, in all states where the system of social habits is opposed to unrestricted increase, to prevent the exposure of children to death *merely* in order to keep the population down. The proper thing to do is to limit the size of each family, and if children are then conceived in excess of the limit so fixed, to have miscarriage induced before sense and life have begun in the embryo' (Book VII). Seneca advocated voluntary euthanasia for the old. 'If one death is accompanied by torture,' he writes, 'and the other is simple and easy, why not snatch the latter? Just as I shall select my ship, when I am about to go on a voyage, or my house when I propose to take a residence, so shall I choose my death when I am about to depart from life. Moreover, just as a long-drawn-out life does not necessarily mean a better one, so a long-drawn-out death necessarily means a worse one.'

With the triumph of Christianity euthanasia ceased to be advocated and interest in the subject was not aroused again until the nineteenth century.

. . . In 1943, aroused by the reports of what was taking place in Germany, Pius XII reiterated the Catholic condemnation of euthanasia. 'Conscious of the obligation of our high office,' said the Pope, 'we deem it necessary to reiterate this grave statement today, when to our profound grief we see the bodily deformed, the insane and those suffering from hereditary disease at times deprived of their lives, as though they were a useless burden to society. And this procedure is hailed by some as a new discovery of human progress, and as something that is altogether justified by the common good. Yet what sane man does not recognise that this not only violates the natural and Divine Law written in the hearts of every man, but flies in the face of every sensibility of civilised humanity? The blood of these victims, all the dearer to our Redeemer because deserving of greater pity, "cries to God from the earth".' The Pope was here referring to compulsory euthanasia but later he made it clear that his condemnation included voluntary euthanasia as well. 'It is never lawful to terminate human life,' he said in an address to a group of Italian doctors in 1948, 'and only the hope of safeguarding some higher good, or of preserving or prolonging this same human life, will justify exposing it to danger.'

. . . The Christian attitude is based on the principle of the sanctity of life. 'The innocent and just man thou shalt not put to death,' says the book of Exodus (23 : 7), and the Book of Daniel (13 : 53) has a similar prohibition. A second principle also operates, that life is not at the absolute disposal of the holder but is a gift of God in whose control it lies. Man has no absolute control over his own life but holds it in trust. He has the use of it and therefore may prolong it but he may not destroy it at will. Furthermore suffering for the Christian is not the absolute evil it is for the agnostic humanist. It may be an occasion for spiritual growth and an opportunity to make amends for sin. There is a duty to relieve suffering but not at any price.

From *The Right to Life* by Norman St. John-Stevas

On Saturday Afternoon

I once saw a bloke try to kill himself. I'll never forget the day because I was sitting in the house on Saturday afternoon, feeling black and fed-up because everybody in the family had gone to the pictures, except me who'd for some reason been left out of it. 'Course, I didn't know then that I would soon see something you can never see in the same way on the pictures, a real bloke stringing himself up. I was only a kid at the time, so you can imagine how much I enjoyed it.

I've never known a family to look as black as our family when they're fed-up. I've seen the old man with his face so dark and full of murder because he ain't got no fags or was having to use saccharine to sweeten his tea, or even for nothing at all, that I've backed out of the house in case he got up from his fireside chair and came for me. He just sits, almost on top of the fire, his oil-stained Sunday-joint maulers opened out in front of him and facing inwards to each other, his thick shoulders scrunched forward, and his dark brown eyes staring into the fire. Now and again he'd say a dirty word, for no reason at all, the worst word you can think of, and when he starts saying this you know it's time to clear out. If mam's in it gets worse than ever, because she says sharp to him: 'What are yo' looking so bleddy black for?' as if it might be because of something she's done, and before you know what's happening he's tipped up a tableful of pots and mam's gone out of the house crying. Dad hunches back over the fire and goes on swearing. All because of a packet of fags.

I once saw him broodier than I'd ever seen him, so that I thought he'd gone crackers in a quiet sort of way—until a fly flew to within a yard of him. Then his hand shot out, got it, and slung it crippled into the roaring fire. After that he cheered up a bit and mashed some tea.

Well, that's where the rest of us get our black looks from. It stands to reason we'd have them with a dad who carries on like that, don't it? Black looks run in the family. Some families have them and some don't. Our family has them right enough, and that's certain, so when we're fed-up we're really fed-up. Nobody knows why we get as fed-up as we do or why it gives us these black looks when we are. Some people get fed-up and don't look bad at all: they seem happy in a funny sort of way, as if they've just been set free from clink after being in there for something they didn't do, or come out of the pictures after sitting plugged for eight hours at a bad film, or just missed a bus they ran half a mile for and seen it was the wrong one just after they'd stopped running—but in our family it's murder for the others if one of us is fed-up. I've asked myself lots of times what it is, but I can never get any sort of answer even if I sit and think for hours, which I must admit I don't do, though it looks good when I say I do. But I sit and think for long enough, until mam says to me, at seeing me scrunched up over the fire like dad: 'What are yo' looking so black for?' So I've just got to stop thinking about it in case I get really black and fed-up and go the same way as dad, tipping up a tableful of pots and all.

Mostly I suppose there's nothing to look so black for: though it's nobody's fault and you can't blame anyone for looking black because I'm sure it's summat in the blood. But on this Saturday afternoon I was looking so black that when dad came in from the bookie's he said to me: 'What's up wi' yo'?'

'I feel badly,' I fibbed. He'd have had a fit if I'd said I was only black because I hadn't gone to the pictures.

'Well have a wash,' he told me.

'I don't want a wash,' I said, and that was a fact.

'Well get outside and get some fresh air then,' he shouted.

I did as I was told, double quick, because if ever dad goes as far as to tell me to get some fresh air I know it's time to get away from him. But outside the air wasn't so fresh, what with that bloody great bike factory bashing away at the yard-end. I didn't know where to go, so I walked up the yard a bit and sat down near somebody's back gate.

Then I saw this bloke who hadn't lived long in our yard. He was tall and thin and had a face like a parson except that he wore a flat cap and had a moustache that drooped, and looked as though he hadn't had a square meal for a year. I didn't think much o' this at the time: but I remember that as he turned in by the yard-end one of the nosy gossiping women who stood there every minute of the day except when she trudged to the pawnshop with her husband's bike or best suit, shouted to him: 'What's that rope for, mate?'

He called back: 'It's to 'ang messen wi', missis,' and she cackled at his bloody good joke so loud and long you'd think she never heard such a good 'un, though the next day she cackled on the other side of her fat face.

He walked by me puffing a fag and carrying his coil of brand-new rope, and he had to step over me to get past. His boot nearly took my shoulder off, and when I told him to watch where he was going I don't think he heard me because he didn't even look round. Hardly anybody was about. All the kids were still at the pictures, and most of their mams and dads were downtown doing the shopping.

The bloke walked down the yard to his back door, and having nothing better to do because I hadn't gone to the pictures I followed him. You see, he left his back door open a bit, so I gave it a push and went in. I stood there, just watching him, sucking my thumb, the other hand in my pocket. I suppose he knew I was there, because his eyes were moving more natural now, but he didn't seem to mind. 'What are yer going to do wi' that rope, mate?' I asked him.

'I'm going ter 'ang messen, lad,' he told me, as though he'd done it a time or two already, and people had usually asked him questions like this beforehand.

'What for, mate?' He must have thought I was a nosy young bogger.

''Cause I want to, that's what for,' he said, clearing all the pots off the table and pulling it to the middle of the room. Then he stood on it to fasten the rope to the light-fitting. The table creaked and didn't look very safe, but it did him for what he wanted.

'It wain't hold up, mate,' I said to him, thinking how much better it was being here than sitting in the pictures and seeing the Jungle Jim serial.

But he got nettled now and turned on me. 'Mind yer own business.'

I thought he was going to tell me to scram, but he didn't. He made ever such a fancy knot with that rope, as though he's been a sailor or summat, and as he tied it he was whistling a fancy tune to himself. Then he got down from the table and pushed it back to the wall, and put a chair in its place. He wasn't looking black at all, nowhere near as black as anybody in our family when they're feeling fed-up. If ever he'd looked only half as black as our dad looked twice a week he'd have hanged himself years ago, I couldn't help thinking. But he was making a good job of that rope all right, as though he'd thought about it a lot anyway, and as though it was going to be the last thing he'd ever do. But I knew something he didn't know, because he wasn't standing where I was. I knew the rope wouldn't hold up, and I told him so, again.

'Shut yer gob,' he said, but quiet like, 'or I'll kick yer out.'

I didn't want to miss it, so I said nothing. He took his cap off and put it on the dresser, then he took his coat off, and his scarf, and spread them out on the sofa. I wasn't a bit frightened, like I might be now at sixteen, because it was interesting. And being only ten I'd never had a chance to see a bloke hang himself before. We got pally, the two of us, before he slipped the rope around his neck.

'Shut the door,' he asked me, and I did as I was told. 'Ye're a good lad for your age,' he said to me while I sucked my thumb, and he felt in his pockets and pulled out all that was inside, throwing the handful of bits and bobs on the table: fag packet and peppermints, a pawn ticket, an old comb, and a few coppers. He picked out a penny and gave it to me, saying: 'Now listen ter me, young 'un. I'm going to 'ang messen, and when I'm swinging I want you to gi' this chair a bloody good kick and push it away. All right?'

I nodded.

He put the rope around his neck, and then took it off like it was a tie that didn't fit. 'What are yer going to do it for, mate?' I asked again.

'Because I'm fed-up,' he said, looking very unhappy. 'And because I want to. My missus left me, and I'm out o' work.'

I didn't want to argue, because the way he said it, I knew he couldn't do anything else except hang himself. Also there was a funny look in his face: even when he talked to me I swear he couldn't see me. It was different to the black looks my old man puts on, and I suppose that's why my old man would never hang himself, worse luck, because he never gets a look into his clock like this bloke had. My old man's look stares *at* you, so that you have to back down and fly out of the house: this bloke's look looked *through* you, so that you could face it and know it wouldn't do you any harm. So I saw now that dad would never hang himself because he could never get the right sort of look into his face, in spite of the fact that he'd been out of work often enough. Maybe mam would have to leave him first, and then he might do it; but no—I shook my head—there wasn't much chance of that even though he did lead her a dog's life.

'Yer wain't forget to kick that chair away?' he reminded me, and I swung my head to say I wouldn't. So my eyes were popping and I watched every move he made. He stood on the chair and put the rope around his neck so that it fitted this time, still whistling his fancy tune. I wanted to get a better goz at the knot, because my pal was in the scouts, and would ask to know how it was done, and if I told him later he'd let me know what happened at the pictures in the Jungle Jim serial, so's I could have my cake and eat it as well, as mam says, tit for tat. But I thought I'd better not ask the bloke to tell me, and I stayed back in my corner. The last thing he did was to take the wet dirty butt-end from his lips and sling it into the empty firegrate, following it with his eyes to the black fireback where it landed—as if he was then going to mend a fault in the lighting like any electrician.

Suddenly his long legs wriggled and his feet tried to kick the chair, so I helped him as I'd promised I would and took a runner at it as if I was playing centre-forward for Notts Forest, and the chair went scooting back against the sofa, dragging his muffler to the floor as it tipped over. He swung for a bit, his arms chafing like he was a scarecrow flapping birds away, and he made a noise in his throat as if he'd just took a dose of salts and was trying to make them stay down.

Then there was another sound, and I looked up and saw a big crack come in the ceiling, like you see on the pictures when an earthquake's happening, and the bulb began circling round and round as though it was a space ship. I was just beginning to get dizzy when, thank Christ, he fell down with such a horrible thump on the floor that I thought he'd broke every bone he'd got. He kicked around for a bit, like a dog that's got colic bad. Then he lay still.

I didn't stay to look at him. 'I told him that rope wouldn't hold up,' I kept saying to myself as I went out of the house, tut-tutting because he hadn't done the job right, hands stuffed deep into my pockets and nearly crying at the balls-up he'd made of everything. I slammed his gate so hard with disappointment that it nearly dropped off its hinges.

Just as I was going back up the yard to get my tea at home, hoping the others had come back from the pictures so's I wouldn't have anything to keep on being black about, a copper passed me and headed for the bloke's door. He was striding quickly with his head bent forward, and I knew that somebody had narked. They must have seen him buy the rope and then tipped-off the cop. Or happen the old hen at the yard-end had finally caught on. Or perhaps he'd even told somebody himself, because I supposed that the bloke who'd strung himself up hadn't much known what he was doing, especially with the look I'd seen in his eyes. But that's how it is, I said to myself, as I followed the copper back to the bloke's house, a poor bloke can't even hang himself these days.

When I got back the copper was slitting the rope from his neck with a penknife, then he gave him a drink of water, and the bloke opened his peepers. I didn't like the copper, because he'd got a couple of my mates sent to approved school for pinching lead piping from lavatories.

'What did you want to hang yourself for?' he asked the bloke, trying to make him sit up. He could hardly talk, and one of his hands was bleeding from where the light bulb had smashed. I knew that rope wouldn't hold up, but he hadn't listened to me. I'll never hang myself anyway, but if I want to I'll make sure I do it from a tree or something like that, not a light fitting. 'Well, what did you do it for?'

'Because I wanted to,' the bloke croaked.

'You'll get five years for this,' the copper told him. I'd crept back into the house and was sucking my thumb in the same corner.

'That's what yo' think,' the bloke said, a normal frightened look in his eyes now. 'I only wanted to hang myself.'

'Well,' the copper said, taking out his book, 'it's against the law, you know.'

'Nay,' the bloke said, 'it can't be. It's my life, ain't it?'

'You might think so,' the copper said, 'but it ain't.'

He began to suck the blood from his hand. It was such a 159

little scratch though that you couldn't see it. 'That's the first thing I knew,' he said.

'Well I'm telling you,' the copper told him.

'Course, I didn't let on to the copper that I'd helped the bloke to hang himself. I wasn't born yesterday, nor the day before yesterday either.

'It's a fine thing if a bloke can't tek his own life,' the bloke said, seeing he was in for it.

'Well he can't,' the copper said, as if reading out of his book and enjoying it. 'It ain't your life. And it's a crime to take your own life. It's killing yourself. It's suicide.'

The bloke looked hard, as if every one of the copper's words meant six-months cold. I felt sorry for him, and that's a fact, but if only he'd listened to what I'd said and not depended on that light fitting. He should have done it from a tree, or something like that.

He went up the yard with the copper like a peaceful lamb, and we all thought that that was the end of that.

But a couple of days later the news was flashed through to us—even before it got to the *Post* because a woman in our yard worked at the hospital of an evening dishing grub out and tidying up. I heard her spilling it to somebody at the yard-end. 'I'd never 'ave thought it. I thought he'd got that daft idea out of his head when they took him away. But no. Wonders'll never cease. Chucked 'issen from the hospital window when the copper who sat near his bed went off for a pee. Would you believe it? Dead? Not much 'e ain't.'

He'd heaved himself at the glass, and fallen like a stone on to the road. In one way I was sorry he'd done it, but in another I was glad, because he'd proved to the coppers and everybody whether it was his life or not all right. It was marvellous though, the way the brainless bastards had put him in a ward six floors up, which finished him off, proper, even better than a tree.

All of which will make me think twice about how black I sometimes feel. The black coal-bag locked inside you, and the black look it puts on your face, doesn't mean you're going to string yourself up or sling yourself under a double-decker or chuck yourself out of a window or cut your throat with a sardine tin or put your head in the gas oven or drop your rotten sack-bag of a body on to a railway line, because when you're feeling that black you can't even move from your chair. Anyhow, I know I'll never get so black as to hang myself, because hanging don't look very nice to me, and never will, the more I remember old what's-his-name swinging from the light-fitting.

More than anything else, I'm glad now I didn't go to the pictures that Saturday afternoon when I was feeling black and ready to do myself in. Because you know, I shan't ever kill myself. Trust me, I'll stay alive half barmy till I'm a hundred and five, and then go out screaming blue murder because I want to stay where I am.

A story published with *The Loneliness of the Long Distance Runner* by Alan Sillitoe

Suicide

The Christian church in the middle ages condemned suicide as a form of murder. St. Augustine denounced it as a crime under all circumstances. At the Council of Arles, in A.D. 452, it was declared to be an act inspired by diabolical possession and a century later it was ordained that the body of the suicide be refused a Christian burial. In some countries the property of the suicide was confiscated, a stake was driven through the body and it was buried at the crossroads, a custom which goes back to pre-Christian times. The last suicide thus treated in England was a man called Griffiths who was buried in London at the crossroads formed by Eaton Street, Grosvenor Place, and King's Road in 1823. There is plenty of evidence that the acts of violence and indignity perpetrated against the dead body were at least partly due to fears of evil spirits released by the suicide; the

161

fears were of the same kind as those which underlie similar actions in Africa and elsewhere. This is not surprising, because it is in his attitudes towards death that modern man has emancipated himself least from the superstitions of his forbears.

. . . The Suicide Act 1961 brought the campaign for a change of the law to a successful conclusion. It abrogated the law whereby it was a crime for a person to commit suicide. In consequence, attempted suicide ceased to be a misdemeanour. The Act made it a criminal offence to aid, abet, counsel, or procure the suicide of another person, thus allaying the fears of those who thought that the repeal of the old law would encourage suicide pacts.

Shortly after the passing of the Suicide Act the Ministry of Health in London issued a memorandum advising all doctors and authorities concerned that attempted suicide was to be regarded as a medical and social problem and that every such case ought to be seen by a psychiatrist. This attitude to suicide is much more in keeping with present-day knowledge and sentiment than the purely moralistic and punitive reaction expressed in the old law.

. . . In recent years approximately 5,500 people have died through suicide in Great Britain annually and about 18,000 in the United States. These figures constitute a suicide rate of ten to eleven per 100,000 of the general population. Non-fatal suicidal acts, i.e. suicidal attempts, have been estimated to be six to eight times as numerous as suicides. Neither the triumphs of scientific medicine nor the rise in the standard of living have curbed loss of life through suicide. They have, on the contrary, tended to increase it.

. . . Contrary to the popular belief, which associates suicide with frustrated love and 'poor moral fibre', the majority of the people who kill themselves are elderly and many of them are physically sick. Their average age is in the late fifties. One of the reasons why highly developed and prosperous countries have higher suicide rates than underdeveloped and poor countries is that the expectation of life is far longer in the former than in the latter. The great medical discoveries of our time have benefited mainly the younger age groups. The diseases of middle and old age still remain to be conquered.

Thus, more people are enabled to become old and sick today than were in the past. This is why scientific medicine, improved medical care, and material prosperity tend to increase the suicide rates. A low expectation of life of the general population makes for a low incidence of suicide. A low suicide rate may conceal more human misery than is revealed by a high rate. The over-representation of the older age groups in prosperous communities is not the only cause for their high suicide rates. One suspects that there are other causes of a sociological and psychological nature. The inevitable social and psychological isolation of old age is accentuated by the tendency of the family group in our society to break up into its smallest units. Prosperity has favoured this trend. For two or three generations of a family to live together under the same roof is felt to be an intolerable hardship. Living in a large family group, which is still a feature of social life in the less prosperous parts of the world, has no doubt certain disadvantages. But freedom from restrictive family ties and disturbing family tensions has often to be paid for by social isolation.

. . . Some warning of suicidal intention has almost invariably been given. Those who attempt suicide tend, in the suicidal act, to remain near or move towards other people. Suicidal attempts act as alarm signals and have the effect of an appeal for help, even though no such appeal may have been consciously intended.

The awareness of the *appeal effect* on the part of those who attempt suicide varies a great deal. Hysterical and psychopathic personalities tend to exploit it while most others do not appear to think of it at the time of the suicidal attempt. It is by virtue of its appeal effect that the suicidal attempt so often leads to a change in the person's life situation. This is probably one of the reasons why suicidal attempts are only rarely repeated immediately.

The appeal effect of a suicidal attempt on relatives and friends is derived from the guilt feelings it creates in them, even if they do not feel directly responsible for it. Society reacts in the same way. The guilt feelings experienced by others in this situation have been regarded as reactions to conscious or unconscious death-wishes towards the person

163

who tried to take his life. There is often ample cause for such guilt feelings, because people who are sufficiently loved and cared for do not attempt to take their lives unless they are mentally ill.

The Only Solution?

Unless society learns to cultivate, from early age, the inclinations on which the positive aspects of social living are based, the outlook is very grim indeed. There should be no lack of time and of resources. In fact, one of the great worries of all concerned with social problems of today and the near future is the use people are making of their leisure time, and there is going to be more and more of it as automation gets into its stride. The planning, organisation, and running of an all-embracing social service in which every member of the community plays a role which is meaningful to him, is the great challenge of modern society. Such a social service would have to provide for the deprived of all ages, that is for the child with a broken home as well as for the lonely widow. It would certainly reduce suicide proneness and suicidal crises, for we should no longer have to wait until a suicidal attempt mobilises social or medical aid.

Today, social work is either a profession or a mission or a hobby. It will have to become part of everybody's daily life if society is to progress not only materially, but also psychologically. The principles, objectives, and techniques of social service will have to be taught side by side with those of science, beginning in the nursery and continuing throughout life. We must match the scientific and technological revolution with as revolutionary a change in social living.

From *Suicide and Attempted Suicide* by Erwin Stengel

11 The power of evil

Dr. Miklos Nyiszli, the author of this passage, was himself a prisoner at Auschwitz concentration camp in 1944. He saved his own life by offering his services as a pathologist. Here he describes what happened when new prisoners arrived at the camp.

The strident whistle of a train was heard coming from the direction of the unloading platform. It was still very early. I approached my window, from which I had a direct view onto the tracks, and saw a very long train. A few seconds later the doors slid open and the box cars spilled out thousands upon thousands of the chosen people of Israel. Line up and selection took scarcely half an hour. The left-hand column* moved slowly away.

Orders rang out, and the sound of rapid footsteps reached my room. The sounds came from the furnace rooms of the crematorium: they were preparing to welcome the new convoy. The throb of motors began. They had just set the enormous ventilators going to fan the flames, in order to obtain the desired degree in the ovens. Fifteen ventilators were going simultaneously, one beside each oven. The incineration room was about 500 feet long: it was a bright, whitewashed room with a concrete floor and barred windows. Each of these fifteen ovens was housed in a red brick structure. Immense iron doors, well-polished and gleaming, ominously lined the length of the wall. In five or six minutes the convoy reached the gate, whose swing-doors opened inwards. Five abreast, the group entered the courtyard; it was the moment about which the outside world knew nothing, for anyone who might have known something about it, after having travelled the path of his destiny—the 300 yards separating that spot from the ramp—had never returned to tell the tale. It was one of the crematoriums

*This included the aged, the crippled, the feeble, and women with children under fourteen.

which awaited those who had been selected for the left-hand column. And not, as the German lie had made the right-hand column* suppose in order to allay their anxiety, a camp for the sick and children, where the infirm cared for the little ones.

They advanced with slow, weary steps. The children's eyes were heavy with sleep and they clung to their mothers' clothes. For the most part the babies were carried in their fathers' arms, or else wheeled in their carriages. The SS guards remained before the crematorium doors, where a poster announced: 'Entrance is Strictly Forbidden to All Who Have No Business Here, Including SS.'

The deportees were quick to notice the water faucets, used for sprinkling the grass, that were arranged about the court-yard. They began to take pots and pans from their luggage, and broke ranks, pushing and shoving in an effort to get near the faucets and fill their containers. That they were impa-tient was not astonishing: for the past five days they had had nothing to drink. If ever they had found a little water, it had been stagnant and had not quenched their thirst. The SS guards who received the convoys were used to the scene. They waited patiently till each had quenched his thirst and filled his container. In any case, the guards knew that as long as they had not drunk there would be no getting them back into line. Slowly they began to re-form their ranks. Then they advanced for about 100 yards along a cinder path edged with green grass to an iron ramp, from which 10 or 12 con-crete steps led underground to an enormous room dominated by a large sign in German, French, Greek and Hungarian: 'Baths and Disinfecting Room'. The sign was reassuring, and allayed the misgivings or fears of even the most sus-picious among them. They went down the stairs almost gaily.

The room into which the convoy proceeded was about 200 yards long: its walls were whitewashed and it was brightly lit. In the middle of the room, rows of columns. Around the columns, as well as along the walls, benches. Above the benches, numbered coat hangers. Numerous signs in several languages drew everyone's attention to the

---

* These were able-bodied men and women who were kept alive (for a time at least) to work.

necessity of tying his clothes and shoes together. Especially that he not forget the number of his coat hanger, in order to avoid all useless confusion upon his return from the bath.

'That's a really German order,' commented those who had long been inclined to admire the Germans.

They were right. As a matter of fact, it *was* for the sake of order that these measures had been taken, so that the thousands of pairs of good shoes sorely needed by the Third Reich would not get mixed up. The same for the clothes, so that the population of bombed cities could easily make use of them.

There were 3,000 people in the room: men, women and children. Some of the soldiers arrived and announced that everyone must be completely undressed within ten minutes. The aged, grandfathers and grandmothers; the children; wives and husbands; all were struck dumb with surprise. Modest women and girls looked at each other questioningly. Perhaps they had not exactly understood the German words. They did not have long to think about it, however, for the order resounded again, this time in a louder, more menacing tone. They were uneasy; their dignity rebelled; but, with the resignation peculiar to their race, having learned that anything went as far as they were concerned, they slowly began to undress. The aged, the paralysed, the mad were helped by a Sonderkommando squad* sent for that purpose. In ten minutes all were completely naked, their clothes hung on the pegs, their shoes attached together by the laces. As for the number of each clothes hanger, it had been carefully noted.

Making his way through the crowd, an SS opened the swing-doors of the large oaken gate at the end of the room. The crowd flowed through it into another, equally well-lighted room. This second room was the same size as the first, but neither benches nor pegs were to be seen. In the centre of the rooms, at thirty-yard intervals, columns rose from the concrete floor to the ceiling. They were not supporting columns, but square sheet-iron pipes, the sides

*These were prisoners who had volunteered to serve as crematorium personnel. Every four months they were liquidated and new ones took their place.

M

of which contained numerous perforations, like a wire lattice.

Everyone was inside. A hoarse command rang out: 'SS and Sonderkommando leave the room'. They obeyed and counted off. The doors swung shut and from without the lights were switched off.

At that very instant the sound of a car was heard: a de-luxe model, furnished by the International Red Cross. An SS officer and a SDG (*Sanitätsdienstgefreiter*: Deputy Health Officer) stepped out of the car. The Deputy Health Officer held four green sheet-iron canisters. He advanced across the grass, where, every thirty yards, short concrete pipes jutted up from the ground. Having donned his gas mask, he lifted the lid of the pipe, which was also made of concrete. He opened one of the cans and poured the contents—a mauve granulated material—into the opening. The granulated substance fell in a lump to the bottom. The gas it produced escaped through the perforations, and within a few seconds filled the room in which the deportees were stacked. Within five minutes everybody was dead.

For every convoy it was the same story. Red Cross cars brought the gas from the outside. There was never a stock of it in the crematorium. The precaution was scandalous, but still more scandalous was the fact that the gas was brought in a car bearing the insignia of the International Red Cross. In order to be certain of their business the two gas-butchers waited another five minutes. Then they lighted cigarettes and drove off in their car. They had just killed 3,000 innocents.

Twenty minutes later the electric ventilators were set going in order to evacuate the gas. The doors opened, the trucks arrived, and a Sonderkommando squad loaded the clothing and the shoes separately. They were going to disinfect them. This time it was a case of real disinfection. Later they would transport them by rail to various parts of the country.

The ventilators, patented 'Exhator' system, quickly evacuated the gas from the room, but in the crannies between the dead and the cracks of the doors small pockets of it always remained. Even two hours later it caused a suffocating cough. For that reason the Sonderkommando group which first moved into the room was equipped with gas masks.

Once again the room was powerfully lighted, revealing a horrible spectacle.

The bodies were not lying here and there throughout the room, but piled in a mass to the ceiling. The reason for this was that the gas first inundated the lower layers of air and rose but slowly towards the ceiling. This forced the victims to trample one another in a frantic effort to escape the gas. Yet a few feet higher up the gas reached them. What a struggle for life there must have been! Nevertheless it was merely a matter of two or three minutes' respite. If they had been able to think about what they were doing, they would have realised they were trampling their own children, their wives, their relatives. But they couldn't think. Their gestures were no more than the reflexes of the instinct of self-preservation. I noticed that the bodies of the women, the children, and the aged were at the bottom of the pile; at the top, the strongest. Their bodies, which were covered with scratches and bruises from the struggle which had set them against each other, were often interlaced. Blood oozed from their noses and mouths; their faces, bloated and blue, were so deformed as to be almost unrecognisable. Nevertheless some of the Sonderkommando often did recognize their kin. The encounter was not easy, and I dreaded it for myself. I had no reason to be here, and yet I had come down among the dead. I felt it my duty to my people and to the entire world to be able to give an accurate account of what I had seen if ever, by some miraculous whim of fate, I should escape.

The Sonderkommando squad, outfitted with large rubber boots, lined up around the hill of bodies and flooded it with powerful jets of water. This was necessary because the final act of those who die by drowning or by gas is an involuntary defecation. Each body was befouled, and had to be washed. Once the 'bathing' of the dead was finished—a job the Sonderkommando carried out by a voluntary act of impersonalisation and in a state of profound distress—the separation of the welter of bodies began. It was a difficult job. They knotted thongs around the wrists, which were clenched in a vice-like grip, and with these thongs they dragged the slippery bodies to the elevators in the next room. Four good-sized elevators were functioning. They loaded twenty to twenty-five corpses to an elevator. The ring of a bell was the signal that the load was ready to ascend. The elevator stopped at the crematorium's incineration room, where large sliding doors opened automatically. The kommando who operated the trailers was ready and waiting. Again straps were fixed to the wrists of the dead, and they were dragged onto specially constructed chutes which unloaded them in front of the furnaces.

The bodies lay in close ranks: the old, the young, the children. Blood oozed from their noses and mouths, as well as from their skin—abraded by the rubbing—and mixed with the water running in the gutters set in the concrete floor.

Then a new phase of the exploitation and utilisation of Jewish bodies took place. The Third Reich had already taken their clothes and shoes. Hair was also a precious material, due to the fact that it expands and contracts uniformly, no matter what the humidity of the air. Human hair was often used in delayed action bombs, where its particular qualities made it highly useful for detonating purposes. So they shaved the dead.

But that was not all. According to the slogans the Germans paraded and shouted to everyone at home and abroad, the Third Reich was not based on the 'gold standard,' but on the 'work standard.' Maybe they meant they had to work harder to get their gold than most countries did. At any rate, the dead were next sent to the 'tooth-pulling' kommando, which was stationed in front of the ovens. Consisting of eight men, this kommando equipped its members with two tools, or, if you like, two instruments. In one hand a lever, and in the other a pair of pliers for extracting teeth. The dead lay on their backs; the kommando prised open the contracted jaw with his lever; then, with his pliers, he extracted, or broke off, all gold teeth, as well as any gold bridgework and fillings. All members of the kommando were fine stomatologists and dental surgeons. When Dr. Mengele* had called for candidates capable of

*The German chief physician at Auschwitz.

German soldiers rounding up Jews in Warsaw.

performing the delicate work of stomatology and dental surgery, they had volunteered in good faith, firmly believing they would be allowed to exercise their profession in the camp. Exactly as I had done.

The gold teeth were collected in buckets filled with an acid which burned off all pieces of bone and flesh. Other valuables worn by the dead, such as necklaces, pearls, wedding bands and rings, were taken and dropped through a slot in the lid of a strongbox. Gold is a heavy metal, and I would judge that from 18 to 20 pounds of it were collected daily in each crematorium. It varied, to be sure, from one convoy to the next, for some convoys were comparatively wealthy, while others, from rural districts, were naturally poorer.

The Hungarian convoys arrived already stripped. But the Dutch, Czech, and Polish convoys, even after several years in the ghettos, had managed to keep and bring their jewelry, their gold and their dollars with them. In this way the Germans amassed considerable treasures.

When the last gold tooth had been removed, the bodies went to the incineration kommando. There they were laid by threes on a kind of pushcart made of sheet metal. The heavy doors of the ovens opened automatically; the pushcart moved into a furnace heated to incandescence.

The bodies were cremated in twenty minutes. Each crematorium worked with fifteen ovens, and there were four crematoriums. This meant that several thousand people could be cremated in a single day. Thus for weeks and months—even years—several thousand people passed each day through the gas chambers and from there to the incineration ovens. Nothing but a pile of ashes remained in the crematory ovens. Trucks took the ashes to the Vistula, a mile away, and dumped them into the raging waters of the river.

After so much suffering and horror there was still no peace, even for the dead.

From *Auschwitz* by Dr. Miklos Nyiszli

To us it may seem quite incredible that Hitler could have caused the deaths of over six million Jews. We cannot conceive such a thing happening in England. Aren't we a modern, civilised people? Before making up your mind, read the following passage:

Patrick

Take the case of Patrick whose mother was unable to face the scorn of her community when she had an illegitimate child *(His photograph is on page* 173.*)* The whole thing came to light because of a small boy's love of fishing. Sitting by the burn catching tiddlers Thomas heard strange sounds coming from a nearby chicken-house, chicken noises, and yet they seemed unlike any chicken talk he'd ever heard. When he mentioned this at home his father told him not to be stupid. Thomas was not to be put off and the next time he went fishing he went up to the hut and found that the sacking which covered its windows ended an inch from the sill, leaving an air vent. A finger poked through and

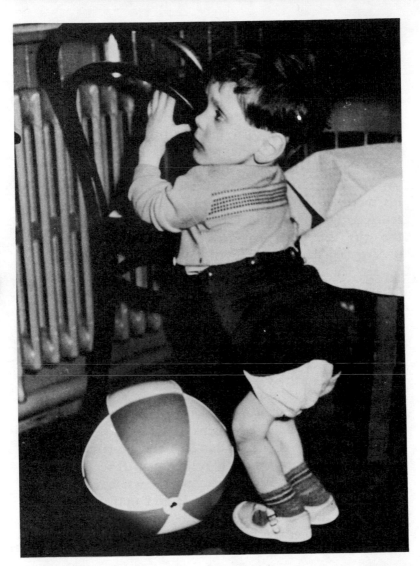

Patrick.

Thomas put his own hand over it, almost like a sign of friendship. Then he ran home.

His father still refused to believe him, finding it quite an incredible story since the field belonged to one of the most respected women in the village, a widow with four grown children. But Thomas wouldn't give up and the next day he managed to pull away the sacking. What looked back at him was recognisably the face of a child, but it was so horrifying with its ingrained dirt, waist-length matted hair and strange chicken-like talk, that Thomas was terrified. He ran, and this time his father did believe him.

When Patrick was finally discovered he was seven and a half years old. His parents were intelligent and he had appeared to be a normal healthy baby when he left the Nursing Home where he was born. He was fostered at once, the putative father paying the foster-mother. But, two years later, the payments ceased and he was returned to his mother, who hid him in the chicken house. This was ten feet by six feet and fitted with wire racks from which the wire had been removed leaving Patrick to perch on the wooden struts. He moved amongst these bars in a sort of see-saw movement, and hopped about in frog-like movements from the back of his legs to his forearms. His toe-nails grew so long that he constantly tripped over them and twenty-eight healed fractures were found in his legs and arms from his falls. Having lived so long in the dark his face was deathly pale, and his shin-bones were concave, presumably in part because of his diet which consisted of crusts and potatoes thrown in to him as it might be to pigs. The floor of the hut was blanketed with layers of chicken feathers, excreta and the remains of the food.

Surgery has straightened his legs and he is now able to walk, although with a slightly rolling gait. It seems unlikely that he will ever learn to speak since he was beyond the age of normal learning when rescued, and until then he had heard only the hens in the neighbouring hut and imitated them. (His mother was sentenced to nine months' imprisonment.)

From *This is Your Child* by Anne Allen and Arthur Morton

The source of evil?

Is evil more than just another word for anti-social behaviour? Here is the end of a letter written by St. Paul to the Christians at Ephesus about A.D. 62. At the time he was very probably a prisoner at Rome.

In conclusion, be strong—not in yourselves but in the Lord, in the power of His boundless resource. Put on God's complete armour so that you can successfully resist all the devil's methods of attack. For, as I expect you have learned by now, our fight is not against any physical enemy: it is against organisations and powers that are spiritual. We are up against the unseen power that controls this dark world, and spiritual agents from the very headquarters of evil.

Translated from the Greek by J. B. Phillips

A God of Hate?

Yossarian, an American Air Force officer, is the hero of the novel 'Catch 22'. In this excerpt Lieutenant Scheiss-kopf's wife is trying to cheer him up. She speaks first:

'Be thankful you're healthy.'
'Be bitter you're not going to stay that way.'
'Be glad you're even alive.'
'Be *furious* you're going to die.'
'Things could be much worse,' she cried.
'They could be one hell of a lot better,' he answered heatedly.
. . . 'And don't tell me God works in mysterious ways,' Yossarian continued. 'There's nothing so mysterious about it. He's not working at all. He's playing. Or else He's forgotten all about us. That's the kind of God you people talk about—a country bumpkin, a clumsy, bungling, brainless, conceited, uncouth hayseed. Good God, how much reverence can you have for a Supreme Being who finds it necessary to include such phenomena as phlegm and tooth decay in His divine system of creation? What in the world was running through that warped, evil, scatalogical mind of His when He robbed old people of the power to control their bowel movements? Why in the world did He ever create pain?'
'Pain?' Lieutenant Scheisskopf's wife pounced upon the word victoriously. 'Pain is a useful sympton. Pain is a warning to us of bodily dangers.'

'And who created the dangers?' Yossarian demanded. He laughed caustically. 'Oh, He was really being charitable to us when He gave us pain! Why couldn't He have used a doorbell instead to notify us, or one of His celestial choirs? Or a system of blue-and-red neon tubes right in the middle of each person's forehead. Any jukebox manufacturer worth his salt could have done that. Why couldn't He?'

'People would certainly look silly walking around with red neon tubes in the middle of their foreheads.'

'They certainly look beautiful now writhing in agony or stupefied with morphine, don't they. What a colossal, immortal blunderer! When you consider the opportunity and power He had to really do a job, and then look at the stupid, ugly little mess He made of it instead, His sheer incompetence is almost staggering. It's obvious He never met a payroll. Why, no self-respecting businessman would hire a bungler like Him as even a shipping clerk!'

Lieutenant Scheisskopf's wife had turned ashen in disbelief and was ogling him with alarm. 'You'd better not talk that way about Him, honey,' she warned him reprovingly in a low and hostile voice. 'He might punish you.'

'Isn't He punishing me enough?' Yossarian snorted resentfully. 'You know, we mustn't let Him get away with it. Oh, no, we certainly mustn't let Him get away scot free for all the sorrow He's caused us. Someday I'm going to make Him pay. I know when. On the Judgment Day. Yes, that's the day I'll be close enough to reach out and grab that little yokel by His neck and—'

'Stop it! Stop it!' Lieutenant Scheisskopf's wife screamed suddenly, and began beating him ineffectually about the head with both fists. 'Stop it!'

Yossarian ducked behind his arm for protection while she slammed away at him in feminine fury for a few seconds, and then he caught her determinedly by the wrists and forced her gently back down on the bed.

'What the hell are you getting so upset about?' he asked her bewilderedly in a tone of contrite amusement. 'I thought you didn't believe in God.'

'I don't,' she sobbed, bursting violently into tears. 'But the God I don't believe in is a good God, a just God, a merciful

God. He's not the mean and stupid God you make Him out to be.'

Yossarian laughed and turned her arms loose. 'Let's have a little more religious freedom between us,' he proposed obligingly. 'You don't believe in the God you want to, and I won't believe in the God I want to. Is that a deal?'

From *Catch* 22 by Joseph Heller

There is no explanation

Albert Schweitzer was born in Alsace in 1875. He became a noted theologian, philosopher and organist (and a leading authority on Bach). Then in 1905, at the age of 30, he began training as a doctor. This took him seven years. In 1913 he set off for Lambaréné in French Equatorial Africa, where he established a hospital in the jungle. He was still working there when he died in 1965. Here is what he wrote about the problem of evil:

Only at quite rare moments have I felt really glad to be alive. I could not but feel with a sympathy full of regret all the pain that I saw around me, not only that of men but that of the whole creation. From this community of suffering I have never tried to withdraw myself. It seemed to me a matter of course that we should all take our share of the burden of pain which lies upon the world. Even while I was a boy at school it was clear to me that no explanation of the evil in the world could ever satisfy me; all explanations, I felt, ended in sophistries, and at bottom had no other object than to make it possible for men to share in the misery around them, with less keen feelings. That a thinker like Leibnitz could reach the miserable conclusion that though this world is, indeed, not good, it is the best that was possible, I have never been able to understand.

But however much concerned I was at the problem of the misery in the world, I never let myself get lost in brooding over it; I always held firmly to the thought that each one of us can do a little to bring some portion of it to an end. Thus I came gradually to rest content in the knowledge that there is only one thing we can understand about the problem, and that is that each of us has to go his own way, but as one who means to help to bring about deliverance.

From *My Life and Thought* by Albert Schweitzer

12 The future of man

Compassion Circuit

One of the reasons why John Wyndham's science fiction stories are interesting is that he uses them for the discussion of real problems. Here is a glimpse of the future as he sees it.

By the time Janet had been five days in hospital she had become converted to the idea of a domestic robot. It had taken her two days to discover that Nurse James *was* a robot, one day to get over the surprise, and two more to realise what a comfort an attendant robot could be.

The conversion was a relief. Practically every house she visited had a domestic robot; it was the family's second or third most valuable possession—the women tended to rate it slightly higher than the car; the men, slightly lower. Janet had been perfectly well aware for some time that her friends regarded her as a nitwit or worse for wearing herself out with looking after a house which a robot would be able to keep spick and span with a few hours' work a day. She had also known that it irritated George to come home each evening to a wife who had tired herself out by unnecessary work. But the prejudice had been firmly set. It was not the diehard attitude of people who refused to be served by robot waiters, or driven by robot drivers (who, incidentally, were much safer), led by robot shop-guides, or see dresses modelled by robot mannequins. It was simply an uneasiness about them, and being left alone with one—and a disinclination to feel such an uneasiness in her own home.

She herself attributed the feeling largely to the conservatism of her own home which had used no house-robots. Other people, who had been brought up in homes run by robots, even the primitive types available a generation before, never seemed to have such a feeling at all. It irritated her to know that her husband thought she was *afraid* of them in a childish way. That, she had explained to George a number of times, was not so, and was not the point, either: what she did dislike was the idea of one intruding upon her personal, domestic life, which was what a house-robot was bound to do.

The robot who was called Nurse James was, then, the first with which she had ever been in close personal contact and she, or it, came as a revelation.

Janet told the doctor of her enlightenment, and he looked relieved. She also told George when he looked in in the afternoon: he was delighted. The two of them conferred before he left the hospital. 'Excellent,' said the doctor. 'To tell you the truth I was afraid we were up against a real neurosis there—and very inconveniently, too. Your wife can never have been strong, and in the last few years she's worn herself out running the house.'

'I know,' George agreed. 'I tried hard to persuade her during the first two years we were married, but it only led to trouble so I had to drop it. This is really a culmination—she was rather shaken when she found that the reason she'd have to come here was partly because there was no robot at home to look after her.'

'Well, there's one thing certain, she can't go on as she has been doing. If she tries to she'll be back here inside a couple of months,' the doctor told him.

'She won't now. She's really changed her mind,' George assured him. 'Part of the trouble was that she's never come across a really modern one, except in a superficial way. The newest that any of our friends has is ten years old at least, and most of them are older than that. She'd never contemplated the idea of anything as advanced as Nurse James. The question now is what pattern?'

The doctor thought a moment.

'Frankly, Mr. Shand, your wife is going to need a lot of rest and looking after, I'm afraid. What I'd really recommend for her is the type they have here. It's something pretty new this Nurse James model. A specially developed high-sensibility job with a quite novel contra-balanced compassion-protection circuit—a very tricky bit of work that—any direct order which a normal robot would obey at once is evaluated by the circuit, it is weighed against the benefit or harm to the patient, and unless it is beneficial, or at least harmless, to the patient, it is not obeyed. They've proved to be wonderful for nursing and looking after children —but there is a big demand for them, and I'm afraid they're pretty expensive.'

'How much? asked George.

The doctor's round-figure price made him frown for a moment. Then he said:

'It'll make a hole, but, after all, it's mostly Janet's economies and simple-living that's built up the savings. Where do I get one?'

'You don't. Not just like that,' the doctor told him. 'I shall have to throw a bit of weight about for a priority, but in the circumstances I shall get it, all right. Now, you go and fix up the details of appearance and so on with your wife. Let me know how she wants it, and I'll get busy.'

'A proper one,' said Janet. 'One that'll look right in a house, I mean. I couldn't do with one of those levers-and-plastic box things that stare at you with lenses. As it's got to look after the house, let's have it looking like a housemaid.'

'Or a houseman, if you like?'

She shook her head. 'No. It's going to have to look after me, too, so I think I'd rather it was a housemaid. It can have a black silk dress and a frilly white apron and a cap. And I'd like it blonde—a sort of darkish blonde—and about five feet ten, and nice to look at, but not *too* beautiful. I don't want to be jealous of it. . . .'

The doctor kept Janet ten days more in the hospital while the matter was settled. There had been luck in coming in for a cancelled order, but inevitably some delay while it was adapted to Janet's specification—also it had required the addition of standard domestic pseudo-memory patterns to suit it for housework.

It was delivered the day after she got back. Two severely functional robots carried the case up the front path, and inquired whether they should unpack it. Janet thought not, and told them to leave it in the outhouse.

When George got back he wanted to open it at once, but Janet shook her head.

'Supper first,' she decided. 'A robot doesn't mind waiting.'

Nevertheless it was a brief meal. When it was over, George carried the dishes out and stacked them in the sink.

'No more washing-up,' he said, with satisfaction.

He went out to borrow the next-door robot to help him carry the case in. Then he found his end of it more than he could lift, and had to borrow the robot from the house opposite, too. Presently the pair of them carried it in and laid it on the kitchen floor as if it were a featherweight, and went away again.

George got out the screwdriver and drew the six large screws that held the lid down. Inside there was a mass of shavings. He shoved them out, on to the floor.

Janet protested.

'What's the matter? *We* shan't have to clear up,' he said, happily.

There was an inner case of wood pulp, with a snowy layer of wadding under its lid. George rolled it up and pushed it out of the way, and there, ready dressed in black frock and white apron, lay the robot.

They regarded it for some seconds without speaking.

It was remarkably lifelike. For some reason it made Janet feel a little queer to realise that it was *her* robot—a trifle nervous, and, obscurely, a trifle guilty. . . .

'Sleeping beauty,' remarked George, reaching for the instruction book on its chest.

In point of fact the robot was not a beauty. Janet's preference had been observed. It was pleasant and nice-looking without being striking, but the details were good. The deep gold hair was quite enviable—although one knew that it was probably threads of plastic with waves that would never come out. The skin—another kind of plastic covering the carefully built-up contours—was distinguishable from real skin only by its perfection.

Janet knelt down beside the box, and ventured a fore-finger to touch the flawless complexion. It was quite, quite cold.

She sat back on her heels, looking at it. Just a big doll, she told herself; a contraption, a very wonderful contraption of metal, plastics, and electronic circuits, but still a contraption, and made to look as it did simply because people, including herself, would find it harsh or grotesque if it should look any other way. . . . And yet, to have it looking as it did was a bit disturbing, too. For one thing, you couldn't go on thinking of it as 'it' any more; whether you liked it or not, your mind thought of it as 'her'. As 'her' it would have to have a name; and, with a name, it would become still more a person.

'"A battery-driven model",' George read out, '"will normally require to be fitted with a new battery every four days. Other models, however, are designed to conduct their own regeneration from the mains as and when necessary." Let's have her out.'

He put his hands under the robot's shoulders, and tried to lift it.

'Phew!' he said. 'Must be about three times my weight.' He had another try. 'Hell,' he said, and referred to the book again.

'"The control switches are situated at the back, slightly above the waistline." All right, maybe we can roll her over.'

With an effort he succeeded in getting the figure on to its side and began to undo the buttons at the back of her dress. Janet suddenly felt that to be an indelicacy.

'I'll do it,' she said.

Her husband glanced at her.

'All right. It's yours,' he told her.

'She can't be just "it". I'm going to call her Hester.'

'All right, again,' he agreed.

Janet undid the buttons and fumbled about inside the dress.

'I can't find a knob, or anything,' she said.

'Apparently there's a small panel that opens,' he told her.

'Oh, no!' she said, in a slightly shocked tone.

He regarded her again.

'Darling, she's just a robot; a mechanism.'

'I know,' said Janet, shortly. She felt about again, discovered the panel, and opened it.

'You give the upper knob a half-turn to the right and then close the panel to complete the circuit,' instructed George, from the book.   183

N

Janet did so, and then sat swiftly back on her heels again, watching.

The robot stirred and turned. It sat up, then it got to its feet. It stood before them, looking the very pattern of a stage parlourmaid.

'Good day, madam,' it said. 'Good day, sir. I shall be happy to serve you.'

'Thank you, Hester,' Janet said, as she leaned back against the cushion placed behind her. Not that it was necessary to thank a robot, but she had a theory that if you did not practise politeness with robots you soon forgot it with other people.

And, anyway, Hester was no ordinary robot. She was not even dressed as a parlourmaid any more. In four months she had become a friend, a tireless, attentive friend. From the first Janet had found it difficult to believe that she was only a mechanism, and as the days passed she had become more and more of a person. The fact that she consumed electricity instead of food came to seem little more than a foible. The time she couldn't stop walking in a circle, and the other time when something went wrong with her vision so that she did everything a foot to the right of where she ought to have been doing it, these things were just indispositions such as anyone might have, and the robot-mechanic who came to adjust her paid his call much like any other doctor. Hester was not only a person; she was preferable company to many.

'I suppose,' said Janet, settling back in her chair, 'that you must think me a poor, weak thing?'

What one must not expect from Hester was euphemism.

'Yes,' she said, directly. But then she added: 'I think all humans are poor, weak things. It is the way they are made. One must be sorry for them.'

Janet had long ago given up thinking things like: 'That'll be the compassion-circuit speaking,' or trying to imagine the computing, selecting, associating, and shunting that must be going on to produce such a remark. She took it as she might from—well, say, a foreigner. She said:

'Compared with robots we must seem so, I suppose. You

are so strong and untiring, Hester. If you knew how I envy you that. . . .'

Hester said, matter of factly:

'We were designed: you were just accidental. It is your misfortune, not your fault.'

'You'd rather be you than me?' asked Janet.

'Certainly,' Hester told her. 'We are stronger. We don't have to have frequent sleep to recuperate. We don't have to carry an unreliable chemical factory inside us. We don't have to grow old and deteriorate. Human beings are so clumsy and fragile and so often unwell because something is not working properly. If anything goes wrong with us, or is broken, it doesn't hurt and is easily replaced. And you have all kinds of words like pain, and suffering, and unhappiness, and weariness that we have to be taught to understand, and they don't seem to us to be useful things to have. I feel very sorry that you must have these things and be so uncertain and so fragile. It disturbs my compassion-circuit.'

'Uncertain and fragile,' Janet repeated. 'Yes, that's how I feel.'

'Humans have to live so precariously,' Hester went on. 'If my arm or leg should be crushed I can have a new one in a few minutes, but a human would have agony for a long time, and not even a new limb at the end of it—just a faulty one, if he is lucky. That isn't as bad as it used to be because in designing us you learned how to make good arms and legs, much stronger and better than the old ones. People would be much more sensible to have a weak arm or leg replaced at once, but they don't seem to want to if they can possibly keep the old ones.'

'You mean they can be grafted on? I didn't know that,' Janet said. 'I wish it were only arms or legs that's wrong with me. I don't think I would hesitate. . . .' She sighed. 'The doctor wasn't encouraging this morning, Hester. You heard what he said? I've been losing ground: must rest more. I don't believe he does expect me to get any stronger. He was just trying to cheer me up before. . . . He had a funny sort of look after he'd examined me. . . . But all he said was rest. What's the good of being alive if it's only rest—

rest—rest. . . .? And there's poor George. What sort of a life is it for him, and he's so patient with me, so sweet. . . . I'd rather anything than go on feebly like this. I'd sooner die. . . .'

Janet went on talking, more to herself than to the patient Hester standing by. She talked herself into tears. Then, presently, she looked up.

'Oh, Hester, if you were human I couldn't bear it; I think I'd hate you for being so strong and so well—but I don't, Hester. You're so kind and so patient when I'm silly, like this. I believe you'd cry with me to keep me company if you could.'

'I would if I could,' the robot agreed. 'My compassion-circuit—'

'Oh, no!' Janet protested. 'It can't be just that. You've a heart somewhere, Hester. You must have.'

'I expect it is more reliable than a heart,' said Hester.

She stepped a little closer, stooped down, and lifted Janet up as if she weighed nothing at all.

'You've tired yourself out, Janet, dear,' she told her. 'I'll take you upstairs; you'll be able to sleep a little before he gets back.'

Janet could feel the robot's arms cold through her dress, but the coldness did not trouble her any more, she was aware only that they were strong, protecting arms around her. She said:

'Oh, Hester, you are such a comfort, you *know* what I ought to do.' She paused, then she added miserably: 'I know what he thinks—the doctor, I mean. I could see it. He just thinks I'm going to go on getting weaker and weaker until one day I'll fade away and die. . . . I said I'd sooner die . . . but I wouldn't, Hester. I don't want to die. . . .'

The robot rocked her a little, as if she were a child.

'There, there, dear. It's not as bad as that—nothing like,' she told her. 'You mustn't think about dying. And you mustn't cry any more, it's not good for you, you know. Besides, you don't want him to see you've been crying.'

'I'll try not to,' agreed Janet obediently, as Hester carried her out of the room and up the stairs.

The hospital reception-robot looked up from the desk.

'My wife,' George said, 'I rang you up about an hour ago.'

The robot's face took on an impeccable expression of professional sympathy.

'Yes, Mr. Shand. I'm afraid it has been a shock for you, but as I told you, your house-robot did quite the right thing to send her here at once.'

'I've tried to get on to her own doctor, but he's away,' George told her.

'You don't need to worry about that, Mr. Shand. She has been examined, and we have had all her records sent over from the hospital she was in before. The operation has been provisionally fixed for tomorrow, but of course we shall need your consent.'

George hesitated. 'May I see the doctor in charge of her?'

'He isn't in the hospital at the moment, I'm afraid.'

'Is it—absolutely necessary?' George asked after a pause.

The robot looked at him steadily, and nodded.

'She must have been growing steadily weaker for some months now,' she said.

George nodded.

'The only alternative is that she will grow weaker still, and have more pain before the end,' she told him.

George stared at the wall blankly for some seconds.

'I see,' he said bleakly.

He picked up a pen in a shaky hand and signed the form that she put before him. He gazed at it awhile without seeing it.

'She'll—she'll have—a good chance?' he asked.

'Yes,' the robot told him. 'There is never complete absence of risk, of course, but she has a better than seventy-per-cent likelihood of complete success.'

George signed, and nodded.

'I'd like to see her,' he said.

The robot pressed a bell-push.

'You may *see* her,' she said. 'But I must ask you not to disturb her. She's asleep now, and it's better for her not to be woken.

George had to be satisfied with that, but he left the 187

hospital feeling a little better for the sight of the quiet smile on Janet's lips as she slept.

The hospital called him at the office the following afternoon. They were reassuring. The operation appeared to have been a complete success. Everyone was quite confident of the outcome. There was no need to worry. The doctors were perfectly satisfied. No, it would not be wise to allow any visitors for a few days yet. But there was nothing to worry about. Nothing at all.

George rang up each day just before he left, in the hope that he would be allowed a visit. The hospital was kindly and heartening, but adamant about visits. And then, on the fifth day, they suddenly told him she had left on her way home. George was staggered: he had been prepared to find it a matter of weeks. He dashed out, bought a bunch of roses, and left half a dozen traffic regulations in fragments behind him.

'Where is she?' he demanded of Hester as she opened the door.

'She's in bed. I thought it might be better if—' Hester began, but he lost the rest of the sentence as he bounded up the stairs.

Janet was lying in the bed. Only her head was visible, cut off by the line of the sheet and a bandage round her neck. George put the flowers down on the bedside table. He stooped over Janet and kissed her gently. She looked up at him from anxious eyes.

'Oh, George dear. Has she told you?'

'Has who told me what?' he asked, sitting down on the side of the bed.

'Hester. She said she would. Oh, George, I didn't mean it, at least I don't think I meant it. . . . She sent me, George. I was so weak and wretched. I wanted to be strong. I don't think I really understood. Hester said—'

'Take it easy, darling. Take it easy,' George suggested with a smile. 'What on earth's all this about?'

He felt under the bedclothes and found her hand.

'But, George—' she began. He interrupted her.

'I say, darling, your hand's dreadfully cold. It's almost

like—' His fingers slid further up her arm. His eyes widened at her, incredulously. He jumped up suddenly from the bed and flung back the covers. He put his hand on the thin nightdress, over her heart—and then snatched it away as if he had been stung.

'God!—*NO!*—' he said, staring at her.

'But George. George, darling—' said Janet's head on the pillows.

'NO!—*NO!*' cried George, almost in a shriek.

He turned and ran blindly from the room.

In the darkness on the landing he missed the top step of the stairs, and went headlong down the whole flight.

Hester found him lying in a huddle in the hall. She bent down and gently explored the damage. The extent of it, and the fragility of the frame that had suffered it disturbed her compassion-circuit very greatly. She did not try to move him, but went to the telephone and dialled.

'Emergency?' she asked, and gave the name and address. 'Yes, at once,' she told them. 'There may not be a lot of time. Several compound fractures, and I think his back is broken, poor man. No. There appears to be no damage to his head. Yes, much better. He'd be crippled for life, even if he did get over it. . . . Yes, better send the form of consent with the ambulance so that it can be signed at once. . . . Oh, yes, that'll be quite all right. His wife will sign it.'

From *The Seeds of Time* by John Wyndham

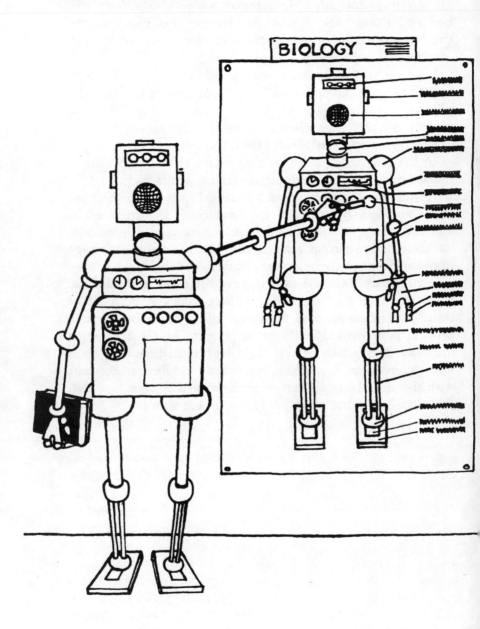

The machines take over

Arthur C. Clarke is a Fellow of the Royal Astronomical Society and also a writer of science fiction. He claims that first-rate scientists never make fun of science fiction and that 'only readers or writers of science fiction are really competent to discuss the possibilities of the future', as only they combine 'sound scientific knowledge—or at least the feel for science—with a really flexible imagination.'

Here are some of his ideas about the future:

When the first large-scale electronic computers appeared . . . they were promptly nick-named 'Giant Brains'—and the scientific community, as a whole, took a poor view of the designation. But the scientists objected to the wrong word. The electronic computers were not *giant* brains; they were dwarf brains, and they still are, though they have grown a hundredfold within less than one generation of mankind. Yet even in their present flint-axe stage of evolution, they have done things which not long ago almost everyone would have claimed to be impossible—such as translating from one language to another, composing music and playing a fair game of chess. And much more important than any of these infant *jeux d'esprit* is the fact that they have breached the barrier between brain and machine.

This is one of the greatest—and perhaps one of the last—breakthroughs in the history of human thought, like the discovery that the Earth moves round the Sun, or that Man is part of the animal kingdom, or that $E=mc^2$. All these ideas took time to sink in, and were frantically denied when first put forward. In the same way it will take a little while for men to realise that machines can not only think, but may one day think them off the face of the Earth.

At this point you may reasonably ask: 'Yes—but what do you mean by *think?*' I propose to side-step that question, using a neat device due to the English mathematician A. M. Turing. Turing imagined a game played by two teleprinter operators in separate rooms—this impersonal link being used to remove all clues given by voice, appearance and so forth. Suppose that one operator was able to ask the other any questions he wished, and the other had to make suitable replies. If, after some hours or days of this conversation, the questioner could not decide whether his telegraphic acquaintance was human or purely mechanical, then he could hardly deny that he/it was capable of thought. An electronic brain that passed this test would, surely, have to be regarded as an intelligent entity. Anyone who argued otherwise would merely prove that he was less intelligent than the machine; he would be a splitter of non-existent hairs, like the scholar who proved that the *Odyssey* was not written by Homer but by another man of the same name.

We are still decades—but not centuries—from building such a machine, yet already we are sure that it could be done. If Turing's experiment is never carried out, it will merely be because the intelligent machines of the future will have better things to do with their time than conduct extended conversation with men. I often talk with my dog, but I don't keep it up for long.

The fact that the great computers of today are still high-speed morons, capable of doing nothing beyond the scope of the instructions carefully programmed into them, has given many people a spurious sense of security. No machine, they argue, can possibly be more intelligent than its makers —the men who designed it, and planned its functions. It may be a million times faster in operation, but this is quite irrelevant. Anything and everything that an electronic brain can do must also be within the scope of a human brain, if it had sufficient time and patience. Above all, no machine can show originality or creative power or the other attributes which are fondly labelled 'human'.

The argument is wholly fallacious; those who still bring it forth are like the buggy-whip makers who used to poke fun at stranded Model T's. Even if it were true, it could give no comfort, as a careful reading of these remarks by Dr. Norbert Wiener will show: 'This attitude (the assumption that machines cannot possess any degree of originality) in my opinion should be rejected entirely . . . It is my thesis that machines can and do transcend some of the limitations of their designers . . . It may well be that in principle we cannot make any machine, the elements of whose behaviour we cannot comprehend sooner or later. This does not mean in any way that we shall be able to comprehend them in substantially less time than the operation of the machine, not even within any given number of years or generations . . . This means that though they are theoretically subject to human criticism, such criticism may be ineffective until a time long after it is relevant.'

In other words, even machines *less* intelligent than men might escape from our control by sheer speed of operation. And in fact, there is every reason to suppose that machines will become much more intelligent than their builders, as well as incomparably faster.

. . . Since this is not a treatise on computer design, you will not expect me to explain how to build a thinking machine. In fact, it is doubtful if any human being will ever be able to do this in detail, but one can indicate the sequence of events that will lead from *H. sapiens* to *M. sapiens*. The first two or three steps on the road have already been taken; machines now exist that can learn by experience, profiting from their mistakes and—unlike human beings—never repeating them. Machines have been built which do not sit passively waiting for instructions, but which explore the world around them in a manner which can only be called inquisitive. Others look for proofs of theorems in mathematics or logic, and sometimes come up with surprising solutions that had never occurred to their makers.

These faint glimmerings of original intelligence are confined at the moment to a few laboratory models; they are wholly lacking in the giant computers that can now be bought by anyone who happens to have a few hundred thousand pounds to spare. But machine intelligence will grow, and it will start to range beyond the bounds of human thought as soon as the second generation of computers appears—the generation that has been designed, not by men, but by other, 'almost intelligent' computers. And not only designed, but also built—for they will have far too many components for manual assembly.

It is even possible that the first genuine thinking machines may be *grown* rather than constructed; already some crude but very stimulating experiments have been carried out along these lines. Several artificial organisms have been built which are capable of re-wiring themselves to adapt to changing circumstances. Beyond this there is the possibility of computers which will start from relatively simple beginnings, be programmed to aim at specific goals, and search for them by constructing their own circuits, perhaps by growing networks of threads in a conducting medium. Such a growth may be no more than a mechanical analogy of what happens to every one of us in the first nine months of our existence.

Though intelligence can only arise from life, it may then discard it. Perhaps at a later stage, as the mystics have suggested, it may also discard matter; but this leads us into realms of speculation which an unimaginative person like myself would prefer to avoid.

One often-stressed advantage of living creatures is that they are self-repairing and reproduce themselves with ease—indeed with enthusiasm. This superiority over machines will be short-lived; the general principles underlying the construction of self-repairing and self-reproducing machines have already been worked out. There is, incidentally, something ironically appropriate in the fact that A. M. Turing, the brilliant mathematician who pioneered in this field and first indicated how thinking machines might be built, shot himself a few years after publishing his results. It is very hard not to draw a moral from this.

. . . If you have followed me so far, the protoplasmic computer inside your skull should now be programmed to accept the idea—at least for the sake of argument—that machines can be both more intelligent and more versatile than men, and may well be so in the very near future. So it is time to face the question: 'Where does that leave Man?'

I suspect that this is not a question of very great importance—except, of course, to Man. Perhaps the Neanderthalers made similar plaintive noises, around 100,000 B.C., when *H. sapiens* appeared on the scene, with his ugly vertical forehead and ridiculous protruding chin. Any Palaeolithic philosopher who gave his colleagues the right answer would probably have ended up in the cooking-pot; I am prepared to take that risk.

The short-term answer may indeed be cheerful rather than depressing. There may be a brief Golden Age when men will glory in the power and range of their new partners. Barring war, this Age lies directly ahead of us. As Dr. Simon Ramo put it recently: 'The extension of the human intellect by electronics will become our greatest occupation within a decade.' That is undoubtedly true, if we bear in mind that at a somewhat later date the word 'extension' may be replaced by 'extinction'.

One of the ways in which thinking machines will be able to help us is by taking over the humbler tasks of life, leaving the human brain free to concentrate on higher things. (Not, of course, that this is any guarantee that it will do so.) For a few generations, perhaps, every man will go through life with an electronic companion, which may be no bigger than today's transistor radios. It will 'grow up' with him from infancy, learning his habits, his business affairs, taking over all minor chores like routine correspondence and income tax returns and engagements. On occasion it could even take its master's place, keeping appointments he preferred to miss, and then reporting back in as much detail as he desired. It could substitute for him over the telephone so completely that no one would be able to tell whether man or machine was speaking; a century from now, Turing's 'game' may be an integral part of our social lives, with complications and possibilities which I leave to the imagination.

. . . And this is, perhaps, the moment to deal with a conception which many people find even more horrifying than the idea that machines will replace or supersede us. It is the idea . . . that they may combine with us.

I do not know who first thought of this; probably the physicist, J. D. Bernal, who in 1929 published an extraordinary book of scientific predictions called *The World, the Flesh and the Devil*. In this slim and long out-of-print volume (I sometimes wonder what the sixty-year-old Fellow of the Royal Society now thinks of his youthful indiscretion, if he ever remembers it) Bernal decided that the numerous limitations of the human body could be overcome only by the use of mechanical attachments or substitutes—until, eventually, all that might be left of Man's original organic body would be the brain.

This idea is already far more plausible than when Bernal advanced it, for in the last few decades we have seen the development of mechanical hearts, kidneys, lungs and other organs, and the wiring of electronic devices directly into the human nervous system.

Olaf Stapledon developed this theme in his wonderful history of the future, *Last and First Men,* imagining an age of immortal 'Giant Brains', many yards across, living in bee-hive-shaped cells, sustained by pumps and chemical plants. Though completely immobile, their sense-organs could be wherever they wished, so their centre of awareness—or consciousness, if you like—could be anywhere on Earth or in the space above it. This is an important point which we—who carry our brains around in the same fragile structure as our eyes, ears and other sense-organs, often with disastrous results—may easily fail to appreciate. Given perfected tele-communications, a fixed brain is no handicap, but rather the reverse. Your present brain, totally imprisoned behind its walls of bone, communicates with the outer world and receives its impressions of it over the telephone wires of the central nervous system—wires varying in length from a fraction of an inch to several feet. You *would never know the difference if those 'wires' were actually hundreds or thousands of miles long, or included mobile radio links, and your brain never moved at all.*

In a crude way—yet one that may accurately foreshadow the future—we have already extended our visual and tactile senses away from our bodies. The men who now work with radio-isotopes, handling them with remotely controlled mechanical fingers and observing them by television, have achieved a partial separation between brain and sense organs. They are in one place; their minds effectively in another.

Recently the word 'Cyborg' (cybernetic organism) has been coined to describe machine-animals of the type we have been discussing. Doctors Manfred Clynes and Nathan Kline of Rockland State Hospital, Orangeburg, New York, who invented the name, defined Cyborg in these stirring words: 'An exogenously extended organisational complex functioning as a homeostatic system.' To translate, this means a body

196

which has machines hitched to it, or built into it, to take over or modify some of its functions.

I suppose one could call a man in an iron lung a Cyborg, but the concept has far wider implications than this. One day we may be able to enter into temporary unions with any sufficiently sophisticated machines, thus being able not merely to control but to *become* a spaceship or a submarine or a TV network. This would give far more than purely intellectual satisfaction; the thrill that can be obtained from driving a racing car or flying an aeroplane may be only a pale ghost of the excitement our great-grandchildren may know, when the individual human consciousness is free to roam at will from machine to machine, through all the reaches of sea and sky and space.

But how long will this partnership last? Can the synthesis of Man and Machine ever be stable, or will the purely organic component become such a hindrance that it has to be discarded? If this eventually happens—and I have given good reasons for thinking that it must—we have nothing to regret, and certainly nothing to fear.

The popular idea, fostered by comic strips and the cheaper forms of science-fiction, that intelligent machines must be malevolent entities hostile to man, is so absurd that it is hardly worth wasting energy to refute it. I am almost tempted to argue that only unintelligent machines can be malevolent; anyone who has tried to start a balky outboard will probably agree. Those who picture machines as active enemies are merely projecting their own aggressive instincts, inherited from the jungle, into a world where such things do not exist. The higher the intelligence, the greater the degree of co-operativeness. If there is ever a war between men and machines, it is easy to guess who will start it.

Yet however friendly and helpful the machines of the future may be, most people will feel that it is a rather bleak prospect for humanity if it ends up as a pampered specimen in some biological museum—even if that museum is the whole planet Earth. This, however, is an attitude I find it impossible to share.

No individual exists for ever; why should we expect our species to be immortal? Man, said Nietzsche, is a rope stretched between the animal and the superhuman—a rope across the abyss. That will be a noble purpose to have served.

From *Profiles of the Future* by Arthur C. Clarke.

The end of the world

Here is a quite different description of the end of mankind:

When the Son of Man comes in his splendour with all his angels with him, then he will take his seat on his glorious throne. All the nations will be assembled before him and he will separate men from each other like a shepherd separating sheep from goats. He will place the sheep on his right hand and the goats on his left.

Then the King will say to those on his right: 'Come, you who have won my Father's blessing! Take your inheritance —the Kingdom reserved for you since the foundation of the world! For I was hungry and you gave me food. I was thirsty and you gave me a drink. I was naked and you clothed me. I was ill and you came and looked after me. I was in prison and you came to see me there.'

The the true men will answer him. 'Lord, when did we see *you* hungry and give you food? When did we see *you* thirsty and give you something to drink? When did we see *you* lonely and make you welcome, or see *you* naked and clothe you, or see *you* ill or in prison and go to see you?'

And the King will reply, 'I assure you that whatever you did for the humblest of my brothers you did for me.'

Then he will say to those on his left, 'Out of my presence, cursed as you are, into the eternal fire prepared for the devil and his angels! For I was hungry and you gave me nothing to eat. I was thirsty and you gave me nothing to drink. I was lonely and you never made me welcome. When I was naked you did nothing to clothe me; when I was sick and in prison you never cared about me.'

Then they too will answer him. 'Lord, when did we ever see *you* hungry, or thirsty, or lonely, or naked, or sick, or in prison, and failed to look after you?'

Then the King will answer them with these words, 'I assure you that whatever you failed to do to the humblest of my brothers you failed to do to me.'

And these will go off to eternal punishment, but the true men to eternal life.

From the Gospel of St. Matthew, translated from
the Greek by J. B. Phillips

The last word

'Who are you?' said the Prime Minister, opening the door.

'I am God,' replied the stranger.

'I don't believe you,' sneered the Prime Minister. 'Show me a miracle.'

And God showed the Prime Minister the miracle of birth.

'Pah,' said the Prime Minister. 'My scientists are creating life in test-tubes and have nearly solved the secret of heredity. Artificial insemination is more certain than your lackadaisical method, and by cross-breeding we are producing fish and mammals to our design. Show me a proper miracle.'

And God caused the sky to darken and hailstones came pouring down.

'That's nothing,' said the Prime Minister, picking up the telephone to the Air Ministry. 'Send up a met. plane would you, old chap, and sprinkle the clouds with silver chloride crystals.'

And the met. plane went up and sprinkled the clouds which had darkened the world and the hailstones stopped pouring down and the sun shone brightly.

'Show me another,' said the Prime Minister.

And God caused a plague of frogs to descend upon the land.

The Prime Minister picked up his telephone. 'Get the Min. of Ag. and Fish,' he said to the operator, 'and instruct them to procure a frog-killer as myxomatosis killed rabbits.'

And soon the land was free of frogs, and the people gave thanks to the Prime Minister and erected laboratories in his name.

'Show me another,' sneered the Prime Minister.

And God caused the sea to divide.

The Prime Minister picked up his direct-link telephone to the Polaris submarine. 'Lob a few ICBMs into Antarctica and melt the ice-cap, please, old man.'

And the ice-cap melted into water and the sea came rushing back.

'I will kill all the first-born,' said God.

'Paltry tricks,' said the Prime Minister. 'Watch this.' He

pressed a button on his desk. And missiles flew to their pre-ordained destinations and H-bombs split the world asunder and radio-activity killed every mortal thing.

'I can raise the dead,' said God.

'Please,' said the Prime Minister in his cardboard coffin. 'Let me live again.'

'Why, who are you?' said God, closing the lid.

Genesis by Brian Morris

Suggestions for Discussion Leaders

This book is a follow-up, intended for students of 17 or 18 years and upwards, to *What's Your Opinion?* which is more suitable for the 14–17 year age group. It is anticipated that it will be used mainly by classes in technical and other colleges as part of their work in Liberal Studies. It may be that some technical students may question its relevance to their own everyday jobs. As one 17-year-old apprentice carpenter wrote: *This type of English as nothing to do with are tread (carpenters) so has far as I can see It is a utter vaste of time both yours and mine and are empolers money.* Students might be interested to discuss this remark after they have had some experience of using this book. In the meantime it might be pointed out that although a student may be an apprentice engineer or craftsman, he is first and foremost a human being. This book is concerned with subjects that matter to all human beings.

The material is intended to arouse discussion and can be used in a variety of ways. You may prefer just to pick out a passage here and there but, if you keep to the chapters as arranged, you will find that they lead to specific discussion points. These are listed below, but there is of course no need to discuss them all. It is suggested that students can usually be left to read the longer passages for themselves, particularly if they have been notified in advance of the points that are to be discussed. However, there is no need to read through a whole chapter at a time. It is often better to be guided by the discussion points suggested. In Chapter 1, for example, the first discussion point is concerned with the first two passages in that chapter so can be considered as soon as the relevant sections have been read.

Academic school-type questions have been avoided but an opportunity for writing has been provided at the end of each chapter. The aim here is to encourage everybody to form an opinion and to express it, and it also gives students a chance to show that they have an understanding of the basic issues involved. Occasionally, though, students might prefer to take the material provided as a starting point for further research of their own.

Chapter 1: The war game

For Discussion

1 Which did you find more interesting: *Flanders in 1917* or *Treasure Convoy*? Which would you prefer your children to read?

2 In *Face to Face with a Titan Missile* we are told that the purpose of the missiles 'is to prevent war' (page 9, paragraph 2). What do you think about this?

3 Air Marshal Sir Robert Saundby says, 'It is not so much this or the other means of making war that is immoral or inhumane. What is immoral is war itself' (page 13, paragraph 4). Is it always wrong to fight?

4 Comment on the RAF advertisement (page 14).

In Writing
Write a criticism of a war story, a war film or a television programme concerned with war.

Chapter 2: Censored!

For Discussion

1 Do you agree with Roger Manvell (page 16) that 'there are always plenty of people about who are keen to get a low sort of thrill at any price'? If so, is it our duty to stop them?

2 After reading how we censor books, plays and films, do you approve of the ways we do it? Have any changes been made since this book was published?

3 There is no external censorship of television. Should there be?

In Writing
Write *either* an attack on, *or* a defence of, censorship as it exists in Britain today.

203

Chapter 3: In trouble with the police

For Discussion

1 Is the poem *Incendiary* (page 29) over-sentimental?

2 In *A Young Offender*, who was to blame for the trouble in which the young man found himself?

3 How can society deal with professional criminals like Robert Allerton?

4 Do you accept everything that is said in *A Sociologist's Explanation?*

In Writing

Discuss the probable causes of crime and suggest what might be done to reduce the crime rate.

Chapter 4: Sex and young people

For Discussion

1 'A large number of boys are active sexually in one way or another prior to adolescence' (page 51, paragraph 3).

If this is so, is there anything that parents or schools should do about it?

2 'The girl is supposed to provide a conscience for two' (page 53, paragraph 1).

Is this true? Is it reasonable?

3. What are your reactions to the views put forward in *What's All the Fuss About?* In some technical colleges instruction is provided in the use of contraceptives. Is this a good idea?

In Writing

A Mr. Prude has written (or probably soon will write) to the local press complaining that his son, a young man of 17, has been given obscene literature to read at the local technical college. Mr. Prude particularly objects to the material in this chapter. He says he does not want his son to be 'contaminated with the filthy language and ideas' to be found here.

Write a letter to the local paper giving your opinion on the matter. This will give you a chance to sum up your views on questions discussed in the chapter.

Chapter 5: Getting married

For Discussion

1 Dr. Jersild claims that 'young people need as much help as they can get to prepare themselves for the venture into married life' (page 66, last line). What form could this help take? Would young people stand more chance of finding a suitable partner if their parents chose for them?

2 After reading *Young People's Opinions*, do you think there is an optimum age for marriage?

3 Discuss the marriage service. Should a non-believer be married in church?

In Writing

Either write a criticism of any one of the passages in this chapter, giving your reasons for agreeing or disagreeing with the points made, *or* write down your ideas for an improved marriage service.

Chapter 6: Woman's place

For Discussion

1 In *The Big Switch* there are disadvantages in being a man. In our present society are there any disadvantages in being a woman?

2 What do you think of Auriol's behaviour in *The Big Switch*? Is there any reason why a woman should not propose to a man?

3 Why shouldn't Andy Capp expect his wife to pay (page 86)? If women claim equality with men, have they any right to expect special consideration or courtesy?

In Writing

Give your views on 'Woman's Place in the Modern World'. Say whether you think that complete equality between the sexes is really desirable—or possible.

Chapter 7: Moving up in the world

For Discussion

1 After reading the Oxford story, discuss what is meant by the 'two nations'. Do you agree that such a division exists? If so, can and should anything be done about it?

2 Is Andy Capp typically working class? Can you account for the popularity of these cartoons?

3 What do you think of *Good Manners in a Nutshell?* Is etiquette of any real value?

4 Do you think our system of education is 'excessively class-orientated' (page 115, paragraph 2)?

In Writing

How important is class in Britain today? Consider this in relation to your own experience and reading. Then *either* defend our present class structure *or* suggest ways in which class distinctions might be lessened.

Chapter 8: Pop culture

For Discussion·

1 Is *Once I Built a Pop Group* intended as satire or as account of something that really happened? How do you know?

2 After reading *Behind the Scenes,* do you feel that fans are exploited?

3 What do you think of *A Musician's View?*

4 Is this country in any danger of becoming 'a teen-age society' (page 130, paragraph 2)? Would this matter?

In Writing

Write *either* an attack on *or* a defence of Pop Music, taking into account all the criticisms made in this chapter.

Chapter 9: Vivisection

For Discussion

1 After reading this chapter, do you think that the end justifies the means?

2 Do we have any obligations towards animals? If so, what are they?

3 Do you consider that the arguments of both sides have been put over fairly?

In Writing

Write *either* a hand-out to refute Mr. Cammell's (page 137) *or* an article disagreeing with *One Doctor's Opinion* (page 139).

Chapter 10: A matter of life or death

For Discussion

1 After reading the passage by Pearl Buck, do you agree that handicapped children 'are not useless' (page 149, paragraph 3)?

2 After reading *The Right to Life*, what do you think about:
    (a) compulsory euthanasia
    (b) voluntary euthanasia
    (c) abortion?
You might be interested in the story of one doctor talking to another: 'About the terminating of a pregnancy, I want your opinion. The father was syphilitic. The mother tuberculous. Of the four children born the first was blind, the second died, the third was deaf and dumb, the fourth also tuberculous. What would you have done?'
    'I would have ended the pregnancy.'
    'Then you would have murdered Beethoven.'

3 'Social work . . . will have to become part of everybody's daily life if society is to progress' (page 164, last paragraph). Do you accept this? How could people like the man in *On Saturday Afternoon* be helped?

In Writing

List the arguments both for and against euthanasia then decide whether or not you think it should remain a criminal offence.

Chapter 11: The power of evil

For Discussion

1 After reading the first two passages can you explain the conduct of Patrick's mother and the Nazi persecutors?

2 After reading *The Source of Evil*, do you accept that evil is a supernatural power? If not, how do you explain it?

3. Is *A God of Hate* sheer blasphemy or just honest plain-speaking?

In Writing

The problems of evil and suffering have been mystifying men for thousands of years. Try to throw some light upon them by describing an act of persecution or hatred (it might be just the bullying of a child or the teasing of a new employee) which you have witnessed or heard or read about. Try to discover the underlying causes of the trouble and to establish who or what was really responsible.

Chapter 12: The future of man

For Discussion

1. Do you think that *Compassion Circuit* is absurd?

2. Do you find any of the prophecies in *The Machines Take Over* at all convincing?

3. After reading this chapter do you think that people have any qualities that machines must always lack? If so, are these important qualities?

In Writing

Does mankind deserve to survive? Imagine it has been allowed one last appeal in the Celestial Courts. Write the final speech for *either* the prosecution *or* the defence.

Recommended films

Chapter 1: The war game

*The Magician.** 10 minutes. A Polish allegory about an ominous military figure who runs a shooting gallery on the otherwise deserted sands. Here, little boys are taught to drill and shoot. Then they are marched off over the dunes towards the sound of enemy gunfire.

A moving and uncomfortable film. There is no commentary but it is helpful to know that the Polish word *wrog* means *enemy*.

Available on 16mm on hire from Films of Poland, Polish Cultural Institute, 16 Devonshire Street, London W1 or from Concord Films Council, Nacton, Ipswich, Suffolk.

*A Time Out of War.** 22 minutes. The American Civil War. Three soldiers (two from the North and one from the South) take time off from guarding a river to enjoy an unofficial truce. We are left wondering what they had to fight about.

A quiet, gentle film that provides an interesting contrast with the noisy heroism of so many war films.

Available on 16mm on hire from the British Film Institute, 42-43, Lower Marsh, London S.E.1 or from the Rank Film Library, 1 Aintree Road, Perivale, Greenford, Middlesex.

We Aim at London and Coventry. 10 minutes. A few shots of war-bombed Coventry are followed by brief extracts from Nazi newsreels showing bombing raids on London, the Midlands and Coventry in 1940, and a V1 attack on London in 1944, to the accompaniment of an aggressive German commentary and choral singing.

An example of official propaganda glorifying war.

Available on 16mm on hire from Educational and Television Films Ltd., 164 Shaftesbury Avenue, London WC2.

The Battle of Britain. 53 minutes. A moving tribute to the British people. This compilation film, produced in 1944 for showing to the American armed forces, makes an interesting comparison with *We Aim at London and Coventry*. But is it really much less unscrupulous?

Available on 16mm on hire from the Central Film Library, Government Building, Bromyard Avenue, Acton, London W3.

A Short Vision. 6 minutes, colour. A chilling vision of the end of the world, produced, by means of paintings and cut-out figures, by Joan and Peter Feldes.

The film is deeply disturbing—but then so is the thought of an atomic holocaust.

Available on 16mm on hire from the British Film Institute, 42-43, Lower Marsh, London, S.E.1.

Chapter 3: In trouble with the police

Children on Trial. 61 minutes. The story of two boys and a girl from widely different backgrounds who are sent to approved schools.

Although produced in 1946, this film is still of interest for the light it sheds on some of the more obvious causes of delinquency.

Available on 16mm on hire from the Central Film Library, Government Building, Bromyard Avenue, Acton, London W3.

Chapter 4: Sex and young people

A Quarter Million Teenagers. 16 minutes, colour. An American film intended for teenagers, using animated diagrams to give factual information about syphilis and gonorrhoea, including how the diseases are spread, the symptoms and the consequences.

Available on 16mm on hire from Boulton-Hawker Films Ltd., Hadleigh, Ipswich, Suffolk.

V.D.—Don't Take the Risk. 19 minutes. A re-edited version of a 1963 Granada *World in Action* TV programme. An alternative choice to the film above, but one that uses interviews with British teenagers and a venereal disease specialist, and gives much less direct information. For this reason, there needs to be someone present to answer medical questions.

Available on 16mm on hire from the Central Film Library, Government Building, Bromyard Avenue, Acton, London W3.

Chapter 5: Getting married

To Janet a Son. 55 minutes, colour. A very well made film describing the closing stages of pregnancy and showing actual births.

Although not really intended for general showing, it will interest and impress audiences of both sexes.

Available on 16mm on free loan from Farley Foods Ltd., Colnbrook, Bucks.

Chapter 5: Woman's place

The Cheltenham Ladies' College. 38 minutes. The story of the college (which was founded in 1853), filmed by a member of staff in 1953. The film gives a clear idea of life in the school. It is recommended mainly for audiences who already have some interest in the subject.

Should girls be educated? If so, is this a good way of doing it?

Available on 16mm on hire from the British Film Institute, 42-43, Lower Marsh, London, S.E.1.

Chapter 7: Moving up in the world

*We Are the Lambeth Boys.** 55 minutes. Karel Reisz's film about a Lambeth youth club (a particularly good one) and the young people who attend it.

Fashions have changed since this film was shot in 1958 so young people may complain that it looks old-fashioned, but the class contrasts brought out when the club cricket teams visit a public school, and the picture it paints of a dreary working class background are both worth discussing. The director's attitude is almost one of pity. Should working class people be pitied?

Available on 16mm on free loan from Sound Services Ltd., Wilton Crescent, Merton Park, London SW19.

Chapter 8: Pop culture

*Lonely Boy.** 30 minutes. A fascinating *cinéma-vérité* record of a few weeks in the life of Paul Anka, the Canadian pop singer, with revealing behind-the-scenes shots of, and interviews with, his entourage. The film leaves us to draw our own conclusions.

Available on 16mm on hire from Contemporary Films Ltd., 55, Greek Street, London W1.

Two other films made in a similar style are *Wrestling*, 28 minutes, available on 16mm on hire from the British Film Institute, 42-43, Lower Marsh, London, S.E.1, and *The Most* (about the editor of *Playboy* magazine), 28 minutes, available on 16mm on hire from Connoisseur Films Ltd., 54-58 Wardour Street, London W1. Both these films are well worth seeing even if they have only marginal relevance to the subject of Pop Culture.

Chapter 9: Vivisection

All Living Things. 22 minutes. A rather dated story (filmed in 1954) about a supposedly famous surgeon's rejection of vivisection after he finds himself about to operate on his own dog which has just saved his young son's life.

Points worth discussing include the credibility of the plot and the implicit suggestion throughout that the aim of vivisection is to cause pain.

Available on 16mm on free loan from the Rank Film Library, 1 Aintree Road, Perivale, Greenford, Middlesex.

Balance Is Life. 15 minutes, colour. An informative, if not very inspired, film about diabetes and its control. It could be shown in the same programme as *All Living Things* because insulin treatment was only developed after experiments on animals. Without it, the children seen in the film would all be dead.

Available on 16mm on free loan from Sound Services Ltd., Wilton Crescent, Merton Park, London SW19.

Chapter 10: A matter of life or death

Back to Claremont. 11 minutes, colour. Claremont is a Bristol day school for spastic children. By means of clips from an earlier film we are shown the progress made by some of the children over a period of three years.

The film will be of particular interest to groups who think that handi-capped children have little to live for.

Available on 16mm on hire from the British Film Institute, 42-43, Lower Marsh, London, S.E.1 or on free loan from the British Council for the Welfare of Spastics, 13 Suffolk Street, Haymarket, London SW1 or The Spastics Society, 12 Park Crescent, London W1. The earlier film, *Claremont*, 12 minutes, is also available from these sources.

*I Think They Call Him John.** 28 minutes. John Krish's deeply-felt study of a Sunday in the life of a lonely old man who lives by himself in a big block of flats.

Is his life worth living? Is it any of our business?

Available on 16mm on hire from Contemporary Films Ltd., 55, Greek Street, London W1.

Chapter 11: The power of evil

The High Wall. 32 minutes. A revealing study that uses a dramatised story to explore the causes of prejudice against the Polish minority in an American town.

Available on 16mm on free loan from the British Committee for the International Exchange of Social Workers and Administrators, 26 Bedford Square, London WC1.

Night and Fog (Nuit et Brouillard). 28 minutes, colour and black-and-white. 'X' Certificate. Directed by Alain Resnais.

Made in 1955, this compelling and detailed film contrasts what was then left of Auschwitz concentration camp with what happened there ten years earlier as shown by film and photographs taken at the time. The film ends with the accused camp leaders denying their responsibility, and the question is raised: isn't all humanity responsible for allowing such things to happen?

Available on 16mm on hire from Contemporary Films Ltd., 55, Greek Street, London W1.

This Is Your Child. 34 minutes. A dramatised account of the work of a N.S.P.C.C. inspector. It is interesting more for the discussion it provokes than for its actual content which leaves a number of questions unanswered.

Available on 16mm on free loan from the N.S.P.C.C., 1 Riding House Street, London W1.

Chapter 12: The future of man

The Living Machine. Part 1, 28 minutes. Part 2, 29 minutes. Part 1 shows 'intelligent' machines in action. Part 2, which can be shown without Part 1, discusses the question whether machines will ever take over from man. There is an intriguing interview with Dr Warren McCulloch who thinks they will, but the complicated arguments make this a very demanding film to watch. It was produced in 1961 by the National Film Board of Canada.

Available on 16mm on hire from the British Film Institute, 42-43, Lower Marsh, London, S.E.1 or from the Central Film Library, Government building, Bromyard Avenue, Acton, London W3.

Universe.* 26 minutes. A 1960 National Film Board of Canada production that uses animation techniques to explore the immensities of space.

A very impressive film that puts man—and his future—into perspective.

Available on 16mm on hire from the Central Film Library, Government Building, Bromyard Avenue, Acton, London W3.

Films marked * are particularly recommended. Many other useful films on social topics are available from Concord Films Council, Nacton, Ipswich. A small charge is made for their catalogue which is invaluable.